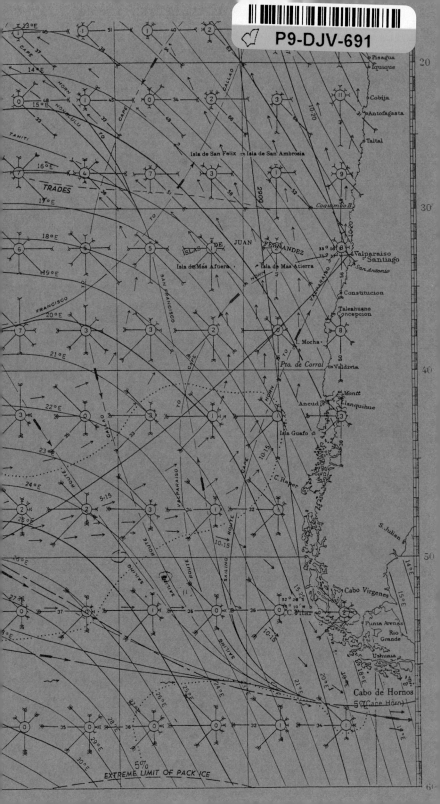

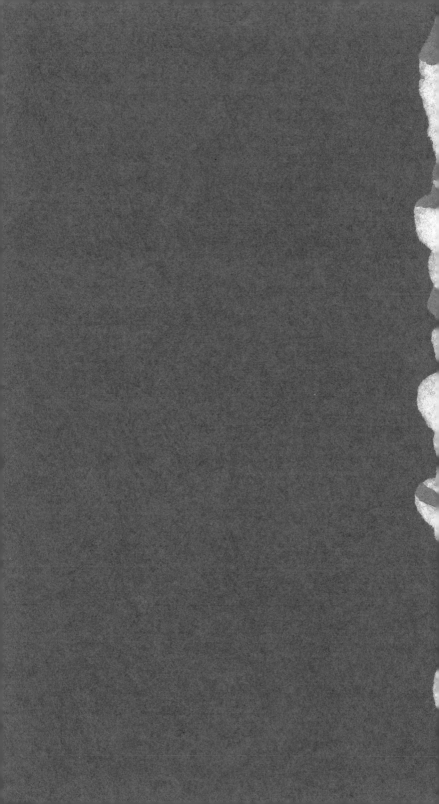

My Old Man and the Sea

Also by David Hays

LIGHT ON THE SUBJECT:
Stage Lighting for Directors and Actors—
and the Rest of Us

David Hays and Daniel Hays

MY OLD MAN
AND THE SEA

A FATHER AND SON SAIL
AROUND CAPE HORN

Algonquin Books of Chapel Hill
1995

Published by
ALGONQUIN BOOKS OF CHAPEL HILL
Post Office Box 2225
Chapel Hill, North Carolina 27515-2225

a division of
WORKMAN PUBLISHING COMPANY
708 Broadway
New York, New York 10003

Endpapers: Pilot chart showing typical summer winds, currents, and
other weather conditions for the South Pacific and the approach to Cape
Horn. The number of feathers on each wind arrow indicates wind force
on the Beaufort Scale.

LIBRARY OF CONGRESS CATALOGING-IN-
PUBLICATION DATA
Hays, David, 1930–
     My old man and the sea : A father and son sail around Cape Horn /
by David Hays and Daniel Hays.
          p.   cm.
     ISBN 1–56512–102–3
     1. Hays, David, 1930– —Journeys.   2. Hays, Daniel, 1960– —
Journeys.   3. Sparrow (Yacht).   4. Voyages and travels.   5. Cape
Horn (Chile).   I. Hays, Daniel, 1960–   . II. Title.
   G478.H39   1995
   910.4'5 — dc20   95–6035
                                                              CIP

10   9   8   7   6   5

ACKNOWLEDGMENTS

Our gratitude to Robert Rubin, Lary Bloom, and Dee Block. Also to Edith Exton, Jan Winburn, Laine Dyer, Cheryl Friedman, Tom Norton, Stephen Jones, Ted Jones, Peter and Katie Feller, the Bergamo, Bicks, and Lorin families, Gene Lasko, Jane Emerson, Edith Oliver, John Rousmaniere, Douglas Logan, Lou Connick, Max Showalter, Jack Evans, Harry Shoemaker, Carole Hyatt, and to Julia and Jack. We are indebted to Felix Reisenberg's books on Cape Horn and to the Mystic Seaport Museum's Blunt White Library.

A special thanks from Dan to Jeffrey, Will, Janet, Ken, Rob, and Julie, and all those who tried to teach me how to spell, but who finally gave up and concentrated on what I was saying. And to Ilene, who hasn't given up yet.

TO LEONORA

Contents

Prologue

DAVID

This is a book of passage, of two who sailed together, rarely more than three feet apart, in a boat so small that perhaps six other craft her length had passed from ocean to ocean at the bottom of the world.

It is a book by two authors, each speaking in his own voice. We occasionally agree on the subject. My son, Dan, writes of a voyage external and internal, a true passage of personal struggle and growth. To me, the account is a love story, the greatest adventure of all. But always it is the story of sailing a small boat, of designing and building her to be safe and comfortable, of driving her across oceans where for thirty days we would not see a jet trail or a single, minute trace of civilization.

As we set out, we wondered: if we could overcome the forces of the sea, could we also endure our closeness—and our distance—as father and son, in a tiny cabin? This too would be a rite of passage.

"What changed?" the reporters asked us. "Why did you do it?" I voyaged to raise my personal and professional threshold for bullshit. Dan wanted another year to find a direction for his life. I wanted to strip away a few veneers and become fresh again, more like him. He wanted to become decisive, committed to a career, more like me. We both succeeded, to a point. Yes, there was change, but not, perhaps, change that would satisfy the needs of journalism or theater.

THE VOYAGE was my idea. "Let's do the big one, Dan," I said. "The Horn."

"Where's that, Dad?" he asked.

What had I wrought? Who brought up this child? I wondered. I tried this on him:

Sailor or landsman, there is some sort of a Cape Horn for all. Boy! Beware of it, prepare for it in time. Greybeards! Thank God it has passed. And ye lucky livers . . . flatter not yourselves that good luck is judgement and discretion, for all the yolks in your eggs you might have foundered had Cape Horn said the word.

"Melville," I said.

"Sounds great, Dad," he said. "Let's go."

Why Cape Horn? Maybe because I grew up sailing with my father and brother and with salts who whispered the great name the way elderly aunts whisper *cancer*. "The Horn can be tranquil," one sailor said, but "The Horn" was whispered.

Growing up, I met men who had been around The Horn under sail, or so they claimed. I met an old cook in a seafood restaurant who had broken his back in a fall from the rigging. How I devoured these stories! In the fading breezes of late afternoon, when my dad turned on the engine of our schooner, *Sunbeam*, to cries of "Quitter!" from my brother and me, I would dive below to read stories of the great voyages.

At the age of ten I dreamed of the adventure—of

Columbus, Magellan, and Drake. Older, I read Dana, Slocum, Morison, and old logs. I began to understand the
struggle and the despair in the simply written ships' journals, in the monochrome prose that could suddenly bloom
with feeling.

> MARCH 29, 1913: Terrible heavy N.W. gale. Lost
> mizzen upper topsail and main lower top gallant sail.
> Got two men hurt. All hands on deck all night.
> 30TH. 6 AM: Quick shift from N.W. to S.W. with
> Hurricane force, with terrible heavy cross sea. Ship
> under two lower topsails and under water. Lost outer
> jib. Washed off the boom.
> 31ST: Wind S.W. Very heavy gale.
> APRIL 1ST: Terrible heavy W.N.W. gale, ship under two
> lower topsails and drifting to the Eastward, and my
> heart is broken under these heavy gales all the time.

So reads the log of the *Edward Sewall*, 263 days out from
Philadelphia to Honolulu, battering to westward in the
grip of The Horn for 67 days.

By fifteen or sixteen, soaked in these stories, I'd come to
love the water. Everything on it made sense to me. The idea
of getting any craft from one point to another was always
valid, always an incontrovertible act of truth. When school
failed me, when job or even friends or loved ones seemed
to fail me, or I them, the water was always there. And so
this curious idea formed, that somehow I owed the water
for its gifts to me, and to repay it I had to go out into it,
into the heart of it, and not take from it only in its sum-
mertime bounty on Long Island Sound or along the coast
of Maine. I had to take all that it would give.

I FOUND this for Dan:

> It is the last word in the lexicon of sailormen. There
> Nature has arranged trials and tribulations so ingen-

iously that in the van of all synonyms for sea cruelty and hardship is the ironbound name of Cape Horn. Winds blow elsewhere at times as strongly as they do south of fifty. Seas elsewhere may pyramid as high, break as heavily. There may be places equally remote and as bleakly lonely. Currents in other regions may be as adverse. These foes the sailorman may encounter separately or in pairs here and there, aye, encounter and best, but always in his heart he will wonder if he could face all combined.

"Warwick C. Tomkins," I said.

"Let's go," he said.

That's how we began, and before we finished, my son became my captain (though I had to appoint him), and I his crew. What changed? A year after the voyage, my wife, Leonora, asked me who my ideal person was. "You know," she said, "a hero, growing up." The faces flickered in front of my eyes—Abraham Lincoln, my father, Judge Brandeis, Lou Gehrig, Franklin Delano Roosevelt, Arturo Toscanini, my older brother, my father.

"My son," I blurted out and started to cry.

My Old Man
and the Sea

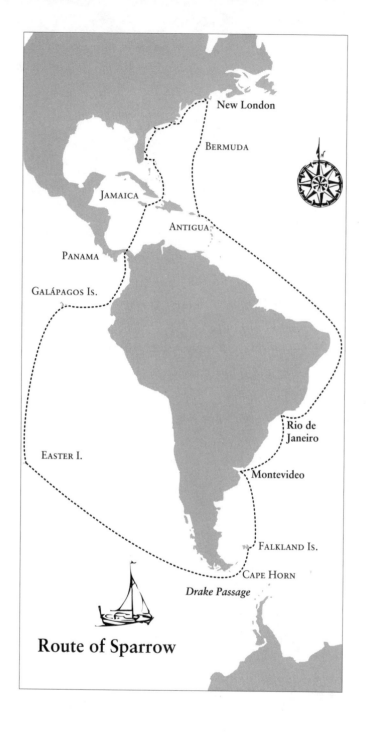

New London

BERMUDA

JAMAICA

ANTIGUA

PANAMA

GALÁPAGOS IS.

EASTER I.

Rio de
Janeiro

Montevideo

Falkland Is.

Cape Horn

Drake Passage

Route of Sparrow

1 THE IDEA

Indeed our sufferings, short as has been our
passage (about two weeks), have been so
great, that I would advise those bound to the
Pacific never to attempt the passage of Cape
Horn, if they can get there by any other route.
　　—*Capt. David Porter, USS* Essex, *March* 1914

DAN

Dad is a romantic. He grew up in a world that seemed open-ended. No one had run a four-minute mile. He learned that Everest was climbed while he was a student, standing through the night in the London rain with his roommate, Norman Geschwind, "waiting for the Queen of England to pass by on her coronation day." Or so he says. That was on his twenty-third birthday, June 2, 1953. That's about my age now. He grew up on Richard Halliburton and read about Admiral Byrd's expeditions as they happened. Lindbergh flew to Paris three years before he was born. Dad's father—and I remember him slightly—

was born when there were no cars, and he almost lived to see men walk on the moon. My grandmother on Dad's side is still alive and she can recite perfectly her favorite poem, which she learned before the First World War. The poem is by Longfellow, and he wrote it only twenty-five years before she was born. Dad was too young for the Second World War, but slightly older friends were killed in it. They all believed in that war, an idea that is more remote to me than any of these other things.

When Dad went to college at Harvard, there was a 20 percent quota for Jewish students, or so I've been told. Almost all of them made the Dean's List. His mother once said that when Jews became accepted in country clubs and so forth, their rate of achievement would go down. Now they are and it has, according to Dad. My older sister, Julia, followed him to Harvard, as he had followed his brother, Richard. They were all magna cum laude. I know it's good to be magna cum laude, but I don't know why. When it was my turn, I walked out of the SATs (to the pencils-down applause of my classmates), and found that colleges didn't seem to appreciate my excuse: "It sucked." I only got into Connecticut College because, while scuba diving one day, I found a 250-pound anchor that the assistant director of admissions had given up for lost. Now I've just finished college, and I'm not so sure the world is waiting for me. But I can work hard, and since I was sixteen I've worked as a counselor with emotionally troubled kids not much younger than me. I usually know how they feel. It's good work for me, the almost-prodigal son, the dark gray sheep in the family.

Dad's ancestors fought in the American Revolution. Mom's parents came from Hungary. They were promised that there was gold in the streets here, and she grew up poor, in Harlem, in a family where they did things like jump on grapes in the bathtub. The passionate closeness that we have comes from that Budapest side. Mom earned her living as a modern dancer from the time she was fourteen or fifteen. She's confused about how old she is because she faked her birth certificate to get working papers.

I love my father and my mother and my sister very much. That's our family—small, close, usually yelling, totally involved, worried about each other, intense, neurotic, and always trying to make sure that the others are all happy and doing the best possible things. As I remember it, the only place we all seemed to meet was up in the bathroom.

Anyway, this trip with my father really starts one day when I'm sitting in the dining room at college during lunch. Dad shows up—he's teaching a design class there that year. (He says the students are so boring that the only thing that keeps him awake is the nude model posing across the courtyard for the Art 101 students.) Characteristically, he has a twelve-volt battery with him—we're always fixing something—and he charges at me pouring salt from a saltshaker and yelling, "Assault and Battery!" I introduce him to my friends, who then politely excuse themselves.

We had recently sailed *Minitaur*, our twenty-two-foot catboat, from the Bahamas to New London, about one thousand miles. I've never seen an account of another catboat making an ocean passage. Partly it's because catboats are one-half cockpit and not the best for ocean sailing—big waves can fill and sink them. We lashed in an air-filled waterbed and blew it up to fill most of the cockpit. We also put a bolt through the centerboard, fixing it so that it couldn't retract into its sleeve if we capsized. We ran into three days of Gulf Stream gale but made it home, and swiftly enough. The real problem was her one huge sail. She performed beautifully if she wore exactly the right amount of canvas and we sailed her well. If not, she was a wallowing bathtub. So I spent most of the trip reefing or letting out the reefs on that twenty-one-foot boom. It was maddening work—hand-reefing on a four-hundred-square-foot sail. We talked about adding a mizzenmast, to convert her to a yawl, which has been done with catboats. That would have cut one hundred square feet from that huge mainsail. But for Cape Horn we wanted a boat that took care of us instead of us taking care of her every mile. It made us sad to think of giving her up, because she was so perfectly beautiful. We loved trolling for bluefish under sail. Once, sailing downwind, we caught up to and sailed through the entire small-boat division of the New York Yacht Club fleet off New London. She was fast with the centerboard up.

Dad and I don't talk well about serious stuff. We are more comfortable discussing chisel sharpening and electrical systems. The conversation in the college dining room went something like this:

"I think we should sell *Minitaur*."

"Really? I have a class in twenty minutes."

"Well, Dan, we can't take her to sea much and maybe one day—what class?"

"Ecology. The teacher's a dolt, but luckily his subject surpasses him. You still wanna sail around Cape Horn?"

"Ha, ha—it's good you don't let him ruin ecology for you. Yes, and I think I know the boat to get."

And that was all it took. Then all we had to do was sell *Minitaur*, travel to England to see our new hull, ship it home, and spend two years building, planning, and reading, before setting out on our voyage. Our plan was that I would sail our new *Sparrow* to Jamaica, where Dad would join me. Then we would sail together into the Pacific through the Panama Canal and then east around The Horn.

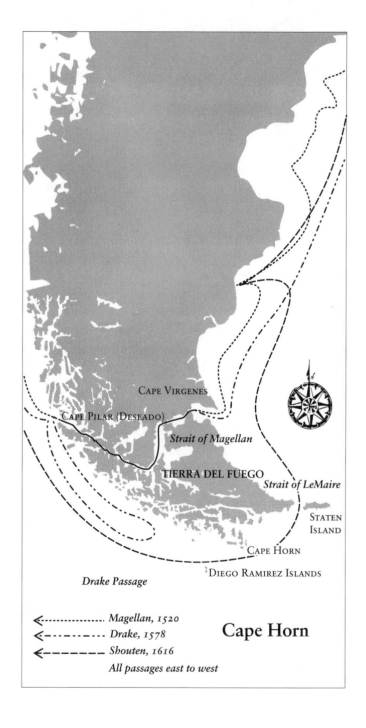

CAPE VIRGENES

CAPE PILAR (DESEADO)

Strait of Magellan

TIERRA DEL FUEGO

Strait of LeMaire

STATEN
ISLAND

CAPE HORN

DIEGO RAMIREZ ISLANDS

Drake Passage

←·············· *Magellan, 1520*
←·—·—·—·· *Drake, 1578*
←———— *Shouten, 1616*

All passages east to west

Cape Horn

2   CAPE HORN

We who have seen the Horn, beating around
it under square sail, or running to the east
past the Isles of Ramirez, low decks awash,
shrouds swiftered in, rope and canvas frozen
hard, screaming fulmars soaring about our
swaying mastheads—we of the age of sail, old
and rheumatic and salted blue, salute the
Horn, our old Cape Stiff.

   —*Felix Reisenberg,* Cape Horn

DAVID

Cape Horn is actually an island, the final upward burst of the Andes mountain range, the tip of South America. If you want to salt up your language, remember—it's called "The Horn," never "The Cape." It is at latitude 55° 59' south, longitude 67° 12' west. One rounds it in Drake Passage, as the waters south of The Horn are called, where the ocean is pinched to little more than three hundred miles wide by the Antarctic peninsula. The Horn is roughly as far south of the equator as Juneau, Alaska, is north of it, and due south of the eastern tip of the United States, around Cutler or Eastport, Maine. It is about thirteen hundred sea miles south of the bottom of Africa, and six hundred sea miles south of New Zealand's Stewart Island, which is below the bottom of Tasmania, the southernmost point of all other continents.

Weather conditions at The Horn are usually not nice. Prevailing westerly winds flow off the Pacific and are deflected down the Andes, free to bend and race past The Horn like the snap of a whip. The currents and gnarled ocean bottom south of The Horn can suddenly mold what

Willem Shouten called the "hollow waves" that bring nightmares of engulfed and shattered ships. The wind and waves between 40° and 60° latitude—the Roaring Forties and Screaming Fifties—fly around the globe, unhampered by land, and pour into this chute, Drake Passage, through which passes the sea route west to India.

India. Columbus never reached that exotic land. His Indies were the West Indies, and the American continent was a wall to the dream. On September 16, 1513, almost twenty-one years after Columbus "saw a light," Balboa saw that next sea from a peak on the Isthmus of Panama. But it was not until 1520 that any sailor passed the wall. In 1519 the ferocious Portuguese-become-Spaniard Ferdinand Magellan set out from San Lucar, Spain, with five ships. He wintered in what he named Puerto San Julian, a bleak haven some four hundred miles north of The Horn. There he crushed a mutiny. In the southern spring he worked down the Patagonian coast. On October 21, 1520, his fleet entered a strait that seemed to promise a way through. It was the day of Saint Ursula and her Virgins, and the headland rounded was declared the Cape of the Eleven Thousand Virgins. The passage is three hundred and sixty miles long, and usually a nightmare, but by November the fleet, now reduced to three, left the Strait of Magellan behind and stood out into the Pacific by Cape Deseado (the Wished-for Cape).

Magellan named the land to the south of the strait Tierra del Fuego (Land of Fires), after the many small fires he saw made by the natives. From the steady and gentle breezes of the moment, he gave the new ocean its magnificent misnomer—*Pacific*, or "peaceful."

In ninety-eight days he was in the Ladrones Islands (probably today's Guam), then on to the islands he named the Philippines after the Spanish king. There he lost his life fighting for a friendly native king. One ship, the small *Vittoria*, completed this first of all circumnavigations, reaching home in 1522 with eighteen or nineteen men. Perhaps eight straggled home on other ships in subsequent years, making a total of twenty-six who survived the journey out of the original complement of two hundred and forty. *Vittoria* was the next to smallest ship in the fleet, but the cargo of spices *she alone carried home* paid for the entire expedition.

After Magellan, the difficult doorway to the Pacific was opened a crack for possession and plunder. It was a setting of scurvy, starvation, freezings, mutiny and desertion, and horrible winds and currents in uncharted waters, but on they came:

1525. Comendador Gracia Joyre de Loaysa, seven ships, all lost, two in the Atlantic, two in the Strait, the rest in battle with the Portuguese. But Spanish domination was established in the Philippines.

1535. Two ships under Simon de Alcazaba. A mutiny, a return home in one ship with a starving crew.

1557. Two ships under Juan Ladrillero sailed from Chile into the Strait from the west. Three men survived.

1560. Don Alfonso de Camargo of Portugal voyaged with three ships to secure the coast of Chile and Peru for Spain. One vessel returned with news of open water to the south. This was not understood as useful.

Then in 1578, with news of enormous treasure coming to Spain from Chile and Peru, it was time for England to try. Francis Drake had twice voyaged and plundered in the New World, and had seen the South Sea from a peak on the Isthmus of Panama, the land described by Keats as "Darien." To see it, Drake had to climb a tree, not as poetic a sighting as in the famous sonnet. (But Keats in his enthusiasm was somewhat in the woods himself, writing "Stout Cortez" instead of "Balboa," or perhaps "Stout Balboa.") In 1578 Drake sailed with five ships, captured a sixth on the way, and abandoned three on the Argentine coast, redistributing their men and gear. By August he passed the Virgins and after only two weeks in the Strait (stopping to kill a thousand penguins for provisions) they stood out into the Pacific. Drake's own vessel, *The Golden Hind*, and the two others were storm-driven south to latitude 57°.

One ship was lost in this "intolerable tempest" before they could return to the Strait of Magellan. Another storm drove them back into open water, where the remaining two ships were separated, and Drake was again driven south, possibly as far as Cape Horn or the islands of Diego Ramirez, where he anchored. Though he did not recognize Cape Horn for what it was, he understood that Tierra del Fuego was an island and that a passage of open water flowed beneath it.

Drake survived to effectively attack New Spain, the west coast of South America, and completed his circumnavigation. In 1581, twenty-three Spanish ships were sent to prevent this sort of attack and to garrison and colonize what are now the coasts of Chile and Peru. One ship reached home.

Sir Thomas Cavendish sailed from Plymouth in 1586 with three ships and completed a circumnavigation in splendid style with much booty. He sailed again in 1591 with five ships; only one returned. Homeward bound, John Davis, who commanded the remaining ship, discovered what are now called the Falkland Islands.

At that time, the well-traveled route to the Indies was south and east around Africa's Cape of Good Hope. Trade and conquest of Chile and Peru came by way of this eastern route and from land crossings. But the passage around the Cape of Good Hope from North Sea ports is about 12,000 miles to Bombay and roughly 19,000 miles to Valparaiso. The new gateway stood only 7,180 miles from Plymouth to the Strait of Magellan and then less than 1,700 miles up the coast to Valparaiso, all with reasonable currents and winds—except for the Strait itself.

This was the age of the great trading companies. The English had their East India Company, established by Elizabeth in 1600. These armed merchant ships fought pirates and hostile navies as they sailed, to defend their enormous profits. Of the twenty thousand European-based ships in sea trade, sixteen thousand were Dutch. The Dutch East India Company was started in 1602 and retained exclusive

Dutch trading privileges. Its monopoly forbade any other Dutch ships from sailing to the Indies by the Cape of Good Hope *or by the Strait of Magellan.*

Isaac LeMaire of Antwerp determined to fight the Dutch East India Company's monopoly by finding another sea route. He established a "Compagne Australe," gathered the best available data, and enlisted Captain Willem Shouten from the town of Hoorn, who had sailed three voyages to the east around Africa. Two ships, the *Eendracht* (Unity) and the *Hoorn*, were thoroughly fitted out and well-manned, and embarked on June 14, 1615, carrying two of Isaac's sons.

Four months out a shock ran through the *Hoorn* and the surrounding water turned blood red. When the *Hoorn* was careened (beached for cleaning) at Port Desire, a narwhal's tusk was found to have penetrated her triple planking.

At this careening, the *Hoorn*'s crew scorched sea grasses and barnacles off her bottom. This was called *breaming.* But she caught fire and was lost. One ship remained. On January 25, 1616, after navigating through shoals of whales, the remaining ship passed through another strait— this one between Tierra del Fuego and an island to the east that Shouten called States Land (Staten Island). Once through this strait, the *Eendracht* met the great waves of the Southern ocean. Thirty-eight years after Drake, Shouten sailed new seas, a route not covered by the Dutch East India Company's ban.

Through heavy gales the *Eendracht* worked westward. The men were dressed in boots and outer garments of leather greased with sea lion and penguin fat. A small fire in the galley below warmed them slightly and helped to dry clothes. On January 29, 1616, they saw a bold horn-shaped headland with nearby islands dwindling northward to its east and west. They knew they had reached the turning point.

Shouten named the entire passage after LeMaire, but the name has stuck only to the strait between Tierra del Fuego and Staten Island. The voyagers watered on the island of Juan Fernandez (Robinson Crusoe's island) and traded well in the Pacific. But the *Eendracht* was confiscated by the Dutch East India Company in Java, and Shouten's claim that he had not violated the restricted passage was deemed a falsehood. Shouten, his younger brother, and the LeMaire sons were taken home in steerage, and his men were distributed to other company ships. Isaac LeMaire's older son, Jacques, perished on the way home, reputedly of a broken heart, but his carefully kept journals had not been confiscated. The younger LeMaire, Daniel, survived the voyage, and the journals were ultimately published in Dutch, English, French, Italian, and Latin. Right triumphed. Drake Passage was open. The new "Compagne Australe," however, did not survive the delay. Soon Cape Horn had become a place of legend, irresistible even to later landsmen like Edgar Allan Poe (from *Ms. Found in a Bottle*):

> In the next instant, a wilderness of foam hurled us upon our beam-ends, and, rushing over us fore and aft, swept the entire deck from stem to stern . . . beyond the wildest imagination, was the whirlpool of mountainous and foaming ocean within which we were engulfed. A gleaming fiery froth on the ship intensified the black night. Sleet, cutting like flying icicles, shot over the prostrate vessel. The noise was so great that it numbed the ears. No one could shout and be heard; we were alone.

Not all of The Horn's heroes were men. In 1866, with her captain-husband abunk with brain fever and the mate imprisoned below for incompetence, Mrs. Joshua A. Patten, a bride of twenty-four, captained and navigated the heavy ship *Neptune's Car* around The Horn to San Francisco on a fifty-two-day passage. She was held up as a shining example in the new movement for women's rights.

The conditions could be horrifying in either direction, but the greatest struggles were the east-to-west passages, where the trials against prevailing westerly winds and currents could end in defeat. Dan and I would sail the easier way, from the Pacific into the Atlantic, and would sail in the southern summer. The storms can be more frequent at that time of the year, but at least the deck and rigging would not cake with ice.

Many yachts had made the passage, but few our size. The thirty-seven-foot ketch *Pandora* was the first, in 1910, sailed by George Blythe and Peter Arapis. She rolled over near the Falklands toward the end of this west-to-east passage and lost her masts, but she and her crew were found and towed in by a whaler. Vito Dumas rounded in his thirty-one-foot *Legh II* in 1943. In 1968, Bernard Moitessier was in a race in his thirty-seven-foot *Joshua* and fell in love with the Southern ocean, gave up the competition, and circled the globe again. Some fear that their personal ability or vessel may fail. Donald Crowhurst, an Englishman racing around the world in 1968–69, elaborately faked his positions while lying-to in the South Atlantic, fearing to round The Horn. His trimaran was found abandoned. Sir Francis Chichester rounded in 1967 in the fifty-four-foot *Gypsy Moth IV*. Bill Nance rounded in our sister ship, the twenty-five-foot *Cardinal Vertue*, on January 7, 1965.

The first yacht to make the more difficult east-to-west Atlantic-to-Pacific passage was Al Hansen's thirty-six-foot *Mary Jane*, in 1932, but he was lost at sea on the next leg, out of Ancud, Chile. Others have followed, including Marcel Bardiaux in his thirty-footer *Les Quatre Vents* in 1950. She was rolled over twice.

Dan started reading and found this, from Vito Dumas's circumnavigation in 1942–43:

> How full of meaning and menace is the sound of those two words: Cape Horn! What a vast and terrible cemetery of seamen lies under that eternally boiling sea! . . . Lives there a sailor, who would not have made a Cape Horn passage in his own small vessel rather than any other voyage in the world?

True, Vito. I could imagine only one finer passage: Cape Horn with my son.

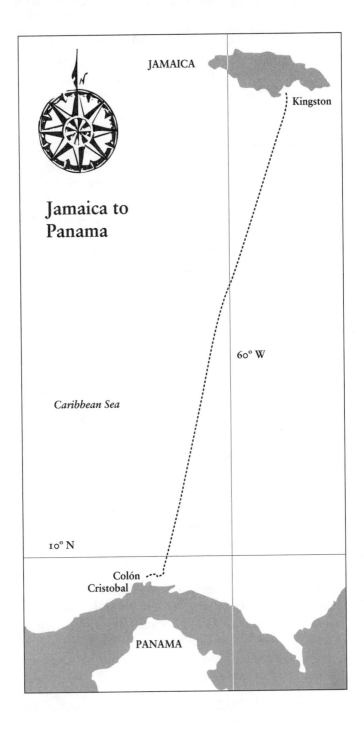

JAMAICA

Kingston

Jamaica to
Panama

Caribbean Sea

60° W

10° N

Colón
Cristobal

PANAMA

3   JAMAICA TO PANAMA

A true specimen of Cape Horn was coming
upon us . . . The sails were stiff and wet, the
ropes and rigging covered with snow and
sleet, and we ourselves cold and nearly
blinded with the violence of the storm.
   —*Richard Henry Dana,*
     Two Years Before the Mast

DAN

DAY 78. Jamaica, waiting for Dad. I'm on the dock.
Three days of chores and *Sparrow* is spotless. Without the
motion of the boat at sea, my body itself has no work and
it's out of tune. So, I'm sitting here, I mean I'm *sitting* here,
waiting for inspiration on the dock, sick of the leather-and-
salt-spray smell of the cabin. I'm writing a journal, and I'm
waiting for inspiration. Instead, I have rum. Another shot
of courage and still I wait—warmer—wait—I grin! I've
gotten us here! This perfect boat, which I made and sailed.
I've got it all down on paper, all seventy-eight days of this
voyage so far, from a shaky start in New London on to right
here. Two thousand seven hundred and forty-two sea miles.

Now I've had three punches of rum, and the edges are
fuzzing a bit so I'm not so "present" with my various neu-
roses. But not to worry—if I go away a bit, when I come
back I'll probably still fit into them. Basically I'm looking
at my bellybutton, and nothing's happening, and I feel
ucky with what I call *land dirt*. "Ucky" is not the sort of
passion to inspire much creative writing. Let some beauty

walk up to me, point and then laugh—now *that* would inspire me. But all I've got is barking dogs, crickets, and a greasy bellybutton.

Highlights of the last two weeks:

1. Getting "busted" by six Coast Guard cops armed to the teeth while drifting in the Windward (windless) Passage between Cuba and Haiti. A helicopter circled, a 150-foot cutter sliced up, and six Coast Guard cops boarded me from a rubber boat. I got a ticket for not having a bell—which I later found out I'm not required to have. They were just disappointed at not finding drugs, Cubans, or Rastafarians.

2. Swimming with porpoises the day I spotted Jamaica. They x-rayed me with their sonar; I could feel it bouncing on my bones. A couple jumped over me and I almost touched a family.

3. Customs in Port Royal. The customs agent had a long "coke nail" (to scoop cocaine into your nose, usually a pinky nail, and, as in this case, painted red) and when I said, "No drugs," he said, "Come on, really?"

4. Right now—being drunk. Not so much a highlight but dizzily fun anyway.

It frightens me that I'm twenty-four and not a little boy. I don't want it at all. Seems like I always need to have something in my life bigger than me to be committed to or I'll go nuts.

At least the moon's getting bigger every night. And *really*, dammit, what's so important about being adult, about being "Daniel"? What if one of my best friends— Joe, or Glenn—says, "Do this, Dan." I will if he means it. Even if he's wrong, my doing it strengthens us both. Mistrust eats at the soul. It makes me mad. Is being *Daniel* worth dying for? I want a cause, a quest. In the meantime I'll do anything. Sail.

Sartre said that the fear a man walking along a cliff

experiences is not that he might lose his balance and fall, but that he might jump—that he sees how in one moment he could choose such an action, so un-wishy-washy. Even when I was small I knew I could walk on the yellow line of a road for miles, but raise it even four inches and call it a railroad track and after years of practice I still fall off every hundred feet or so. What fear!

Can you imagine the power all bottled up in beliefs? If I let them go, what could I do?

I just tried to sit up and had the fun experience of rolling onto my back despite what my brain tried to tell my muscles. I've a grin a two-by-four couldn't wipe off, and I suppose if a girl came by I'd have the courage to say hello.

Glimpsing into my soul—terrible things to keep alone—'cause they're naturally not—takes a lot of work to create the illusion—even Shakespeare—or, God forbid, Freud did not imagine—if you think you're different, you're a dummy. Oh boy, that rum. I give up on writing and have to face a sailboat (moving) that I lurch onto; I must jump and secure a bed for the darkness of sleep, and now I can't tell if the boat's moving or if it's just me . . .

DAY 79. I am of the opinion that the best thing for a hangover is to fool your stomach; I am preparing a huge greasy breakfast of fresh Jamaica eggs, potatoes, onions, and A.1 sauce—all overpowering. The tummy (I use that awful word only because Dad says it's unbearable)—the tummy goes, "Hey, I thought we were 'out' today, but—um—OK," and you're better.

The family flies in today.

DAVID

Sparrow lay, breathless and still, at dockside in Jamaica, unchanged, exactly as I remembered her. A cruising boat is a complete and centered world, and to the mariner's gaze it is the landscape that moves. She was strong and beautiful and serene and seemed to say, "Sure I did it, where were you?"

For a minute I remembered an Errol Flynn movie set in just this part of the harbor in Port Royal, Jamaica. Now, at the hotel-marina, I was standing on the floating dock— *floating! At last!* The small water-motion, the restlessness under my feet—this marked the beginning of my voyage.

My sabbatical, my half of a year of freedom, had begun two days ago on rock-solid land in Denver where we had just opened our fall tour. I direct the National Theatre of the Deaf, and after twenty years, a short break was welcome. Much of the previous week had been spent at a tiny table in a dark theater, worrying if circuit 47 should come on at seven- or eight-tenths full; worrying about a spoiled actor who wanted every member of the cast and audience to know that he preferred one leading lady to another; worrying that the members of today's audience (or their baby sitters) wouldn't last through two intermissions; worrying on the telephone because our major donor, aged ninety-one and with an undeserved resemblance to my father, was concerned (he hadn't seen the play) because his daughter (she hadn't seen the play) reported that there were *two* funerals in it; and worrying, as usual, about this or that grant application at the home office, this or that projected tour. My last official act was to check out of the motel. As I turned away from the desk, exhilarated, my elbow crashed into the right eye of our child actor, and I left him, his mother, and the motel as the shiner started to bloom.

Now I'm here to share with my son the simpler worries of staying alive.

SPARROW. She's aptly named. Why so small? Why just a twenty-five-foot package to carry us to the bottom of the world? Because this is as big a boat as we could afford to perfect, as we understood that inexact word. Every foot of length counts, and more than once: a mast increases more than a foot for every foot of the length of a hull; lines that go up a taller mast must be longer to come down; costly sails increase geometrically in area; slightly heavier anchors need slightly heavier chain, which requires a slightly heavier winch, and so forth. Dan and I shared a desire for a boat that one of us could strip of canvas in less than a minute in suddenly bad winds.

A boat of twenty-five feet (and seven and one-half inches, *Sparrow*'s designed length; I've never checked this) is still small enough to be easily pushed in and out of docks or towed by an oar-powered dinghy. With only four and one-half feet stretching down from the water surface to the bottom of her keel, you could stand next to her and push should you be stuck on a sandbank. (If it's a mudbank, you push yourself into the mud.) No costly engine, no gasoline. Marine engines, cooled by corrosive saltwater, need a lot of fussing, and in a boat this size they sit exactly where you need space in the galley. She feels big below without an engine.

But something more than all that made us choose *Sparrow*. It's how you feel in your bones about a small boat. Dan and I sailed a beautiful nine-foot Halcyon dinghy from Miami to West End in the Bahamas, and the tough, pretty cockle seemed to jump toward the wind off the crests of the steep six-foot Gulf Stream waves. We didn't sail those waves, we sailed the smaller waves—the wavelets—that formed them. There's something perversely snug about being that tight to the water, to every wrinkle in its skin, like a chip of wood or a corked bottle.

I've sailed for most of my life. My school vacations just before the Second World War were spent on *Sunbeam*, a sixty-foot wooden schooner designed by John Alden and built in Bath, Maine. Once in a storm near Bermuda, an old salt hero of mine said he didn't trust the twenty-five-year-old boat. After that, every healthy creak became a frightening premonition. I felt helpless. I pictured the ultimate nightmare and the control we wouldn't have. When you bail a hundred pre-coronary buckets out of a small ship, it makes a difference. Not so with a swamped big ship. And if a small ship somersaults forward or rolls around sideways, I have more confidence that it will come up with the mast still on and the hatches intact. Above all, what you want in a boat is a feeling, a bond, a marriage, and mere measurements, numbers, and specifications don't change that.

It was not only the size, but the design, and I knew the boat for us. At the slightly larger size of twenty-eight feet you can find a good range of choices, and I'd seen two good-looking hulls even smaller than *Sparrow*. But I wanted to show Dan a Vertue — a classic design that's held up for fifty years. I learned that they were being made in fiberglass. Wood, alas, is too time-consuming for us to maintain at today's pace, and the craftsmen who could help us are scarce and costly.

After a long-saved-for family trip down the Nile, we stopped in London and drove down to Portsmouth to look at hull #005, the fifth of the new issue. Building had been stopped because of the bankruptcy of Westerly, a large yacht manufacturer. Number 005 sat in an immense hangar-style shed amid many other hulls in various stages of undress. Smaller than most, you saw her immediately; her full curves stopped the eye among the fin-keeled anorexics. Scattered under her were uninstalled plywood cabinets and her water tanks, like broken eggshells under a hen.

With your eyes you can feel the shape of the sea on a boat. A boat hull is the reverse image of the water: the sea is the surface of the constantly shifting, flowing hole that a boat plows in the water. The vision of this movement, even in that shed, was glorious to me. Feeling the hull in water with my eyes reminded me of a favorite exercise for my drawing students—to draw not the outline of the model, but the profile edge of the space she interrupts, as if her shape is the one piece missing in a jigsaw puzzle.

Of course we've learned since 1936, when the first of almost two hundred wooden Vertues was built. New computer-developed forms are towed as models in tanks, like airplane hulls that sit in wind tunnels while the airstream is filmed. With even newer computer developments, they may not even have to be towed. The Vertue has the traditional hull of the pilot and fishing boats that worked the Bristol and English channels in appalling weather, hulls developed by generations of whittlers stroking the surfaces with hand and eye. The legendary Laurent Giles designed her, and you knew it in her overall shape and in the details. The bow, imagined plunging down into a wave, was not so bluff that it would pound on the water, nor so fine that it would slice down deeply and scoop up ocean to charge back and flush you out of the cockpit. The stern was cut off to reduce length, but she was full enough in the hips to hold the buoyant air that would lift her in following seas.

I stood in reverie; Dan thumped the fiberglass skin—not just tire-kicking, but looking for thin spots. It was his way of overcoming the moment. The foreman appeared and toed the two stainless steel water tanks. "All ready to pop in!" he volunteered in a distinct and, it turned out, memorable turn of phrase.

We climbed aboard and the brochures came to life. Much would have to be done. The cabinetwork wasn't up to sea standards: bitty hinges screwed into the edges of three-eighths-inch plywood cupboard doors. But the cabin form was right, and we could put in our own seagoing interior.

We bought the hull as it was and arranged to have it shipped back to the United States in the spring. If anything, it was more finished than we wanted, with commitments that we would not have made, such as preparations for a propeller shaft and underwater openings for the toilet; we would have preferred a vessel with no openings below the waterline. We were given her plans, and we returned home to Connecticut. We started to build in January. We built the rudder blade from two inches of marine plywood, tapered and fiberglass covered, with two more inches of oak reinforcement on each side for the rudder post. We made wood models for the fittings that would hinge it, and we had them cast in bronze by a foundry in nearby Mystic. We made a grating for the cockpit floor and laminated a sweetly curved tiller handle. We fashioned hatches and the small doors from the cockpit to the cabin below.

She first arrived in New London by truck on an April morning. I jumped—only two or three jumps, and perhaps no one saw me—but, yes, jumps, the way little girls jump. She was an all-white sculpture, a sea-stroked shape, and the ungarnished hull and deck looked like the Ivory soap carvings I made as a boy.

Everything that we had made fit perfectly, and we kept on going. We spent hours in supply stores and with catalogs, and the dialogue continued.

"Too small, Dad."

"Dan, you'll sink her with that weight."

"Dad, it's just one cleat."

"Sure, to starboard, what about the one to port?"

"Well, she'll sink evenly."

We got tired of all the bo-ho nautical terms, and sometimes even now we say we're going downstairs, from the back porch into the kitchen (on the left), then through the living room on the way to the front (the pointy end).

For two years we worked nights and weekends, stealing time when we could from college or work. In winter she was dockside in a small marina next to the local sewage settling plant, where the water rarely froze. We worked on her interior there, even when the wind blew the wrong way. A small electric heater kept our fingers moving. I developed an allergy to teak dust and my eyes puffed when I sanded. We made oval openings for bow eyes and for scuppers. When we cut through the fiberglass for these, we saw an unsatisfactory connection between the hull and the deck, and Dan spent four uncomfortable weeks on his back at our summer anchorage, reinforcing this long joining with three more layers of fiberglass matting. We ripped out finished lockers and the ceiling liner to find unreinforced deck attachment positions for the shrouds, the cables that support the mast from side to side. This was disconcerting. The hull itself had a Lloyd's rating, which meant that good-as-gold Lloyd's of London had supervised building to ensure quality. The architect, builder, or owner could have even paid for a higher approval rating by having a Lloyd's crew test-sail the finished vessel. In our case, the scrawled signatures on our check-off sheet approved items that did not even appear on the plans, and this hidden area was omitted. A boat builder, like a house carpenter, can have some leeway in detail—or perhaps someone stepped out to lunch, or high standards were met on the first few boats and then eased. The mast might have come down in a medium breeze. A sobering thought. No one would be standing by us a thousand miles at sea, and that had to be in our minds now. We became proud of every screw and bolt.

We built almost everything below, but at a boat show I spotted a neat teak binocular box that we could mount just inside the cabin, where we could reach it from the cockpit, and it looked quite pretty. And we had to make the water tanks. The tanks ("All ready to pop in!") had not arrived with *Sparrow*. I wrote to Westerly and received a blue-ribbon addition to anyone's collection of bizarre letters.

I am afraid that these have been overlooked as they did not explicitly appear on the Contract and unfortunately they have been sold to another Vertue owner who has just taken delivery of his boat . . .

Against instinct I sent a calm and measured reply. I reminded the foreman of his remark and argued that the tanks had been presented to us as custom-made parts of our boat, that they were knowingly a part of the negotiation and had clearly been sold twice. Westerly agreed with deceptive ease to my argument, and although the settlement was shamefully small, I rationalized that I was keeping on good terms with the builder. A waste of time. Westerly never paid. My instinct was right—I should have cussed them out early and saved the time and energy. Peter Feller, Jr., made new ones beautifully in his stage machinery shop.

We built and built, and in the summer of 1983, more than a year after she arrived, we sailed her for a few hours, looking at her new sails, by Arun. Then we went right back to building. There was a small incident during that sail that made an impact on Dan. After viewing *Sparrow* from our rubber dinghy, I had difficulty climbing back on board because of unfamiliar obstacles that Dan may not have seen clearly. I saw for the first time, in just a flicker across his face, his distress that I was becoming old.

The work itself was joyful. The good craftsmen who made pieces for us out of bronze and stainless steel caught our enthusiasm. Only one, a rigger from Essex, didn't appear at the carefully appointed and triple-checked hour, as the crane at Burr's dock and six of us awaited his arrival to supervise the stepping of our fine Kemp mast. "Frightfully busy day," he stated cheerfully on the phone.

We put on handrails, which were bolted through the cabin top and always curved for strength. Winches went on, and the cleats were carefully angled for two right-handers. The deck pulleys were seated on teak pads shaped to present just the right angle for the turn of the line. We designed a high main traveller (I like the British name, "horse") to lift the main sheet above the lifelines, to keep it from rubbing when *Sparrow* sailed downwind. Old-fashioned in these days of tracks, it would work well and would be an extra rail to keep us from being flushed backward out of the cockpit.

Everything we wanted went into the deck layout. We installed long tracks to vary the placement of deck blocks (pulleys); each bolt was secured—Dan below catching the nut, I above with the screwdriver. Most lines led to the cockpit, with attention to where the coils would fall. We designed a high and roomy bow pulpit—the half circle of waist-high railing that keeps you on board when handling jibs and the anchor.

The tiller, which passed through the top of the rudder post, was held in place by a cello peg. The last things we built, the morning she sailed from Burr's Yacht Haven in New London, were the steps down into the deep cabin— two triangular steps tucked away. A conventional ladder would have taken up too much room. Maybe they'd help, maybe we'd use them. One would double as a good cutting board for the galley, and one as a bit of a seat. Maybe we'd be walking down the walls or on each other's shoulders, scrambling in and out when she was jumping at sea, when we'd feel like objects in a lady's handbag as she banged it on the head of a robber . . .

AND NOW, in Jamaica, I was finally about to go aboard. The small vessel stirred. "Dan," I called, and ran the few steps on the floating dock. He appeared at the hatchway. "Hi, Dad." What a thrill to see him. He looked like hell.

DAN

After Dad, Mom flies in with a family friend and our favorite aunt, Elaine. Then my older sister, Julia, with her very close friend Jack. We give Tiger, the ship's kitten and soon-to-be ship's cat, a bath in a bucket. Dad gets an on-dock haircut from Julia. They worry about air conditioning in their rooms. We eat too much, drive through beautiful rain forests and over coffee mountains.

During their resting time, Dad and I cram in all sorts of work: reinforcements, more non-slip paint, and clever latches. We have several solutions to all the foreseen problems like losing the mast, a hatch breaking, etc. There's extra wood stowed forward for this. There's a problem with the windlass, an important winch attached to the foredeck. It winds in the anchor chain, and its leverage and gearing let you hand-crank hundreds of pounds of anchor to boat, or boat to anchor. I rebuild it again and am so angry at the company responsible! I'm sure that the Simpson-Lawrence Sea-Horse SL-513 is improved by now, but don't buy the model unless you like taking things apart. The clutch has delicate parts. A manual winch with delicate parts! I've phoned them a few times. The boss: "Strange, that's the first complaint . . ." Once I caught the foreman when the boss was out. "Yeah, I'm up to my butt repairing that model." I'm thinking of using wing nuts on its bolts so I can remove it quickly for repair. The first-ever anchor winch bolted on by wing nuts.

It is Yom Kippur, and we go to an ancient synagogue here in Jamaica. Jack is the most informed about our traditions and points out that in this old style, the reading platform and the ark that holds the scrolls are at opposite ends of the room. The floor is sand, and when there is a procession of men carrying the scrolls to the platform to be read, it's like the journey across the desert.

On the way home all seven of us and the driver crowd into one taxi. We are stopped by a crowd at the edge of a downtown Kingston square. Angry faces fill the windows. "Who's in there? Where you going, white people?" The driver is petrified and can't move or talk. The car starts rocking. Suddenly a huge man in a flowered shirt pulls back another whose face is jammed through the car window. There is a short scuffle and angry words we can't make out. The crowd divides and we drive on.

The next morning it all becomes clear! I learn from Mom that I was ten days overdue—I was *induced*, forced out before I was ready to be born—I *never wanted to leave!* She explains that it was a Friday afternoon, and the doctor brought in three women and induced all three. My life's voyage, begun on a Friday.

We all crowd on *Sparrow* and sail in a gentle breeze at dusk and moonrise. A nice harbor sail that seems trite at the moment, but *Sparrow* shrugs her shoulders and lets it happen. Aunt Elaine and our friend fly off, and on the last night together, Julia turns off the presidential debate and Jack tells us they want to marry.

The family is on various airplanes and away, back to their city lives after we've gotten all sad and teary by the airport x-ray machines. Now it's just me 'n' Dad; he's full of excitement, and I play casual. We shop, and although we find other things we turn up just one onion. That's not enough, but the hotel manager, Marlaine, gives us a whole big bunch and we're happy. As we load on the groceries, Marlaine asks, "No woman?"

"No," Dad says, "I'm too old, my son is fed up, and the cat's too young to be either."

We search through the small town, close to midnight, and find the customs officer in a bar. He clears us under a forty-watt bulb in the little office with that West Indies style of crumbling cement. Why does concrete fall apart on these islands? Dad thinks it's because they use beach sand and each grain is worn smooth—no grip. He's invented answers to all my questions since I could talk.

We give the officer the last of our Jamaican money, thirty cents short, and sail away under a full moon.

DAVID

"Dan—we're off! I mean *I'm* off! I mean here we are together! Wow, those mountains. Oh, Dan, she moves so beautifully. Due south! Look at that sun—in white mist— it's like the moon doing an encore! Wow, Dan, here we go! On to the Pacific!"

"Sure, Dad."

October 9 was my first full day at sea and the eighty-seventh day of Dan's voyage—now also mine. Dan wore nothing. I tried that and was quickly burned in cracks and crevices that stabbed me with pain when I crawled in or out of the tiny hatch.

Around noon on our second day, we were still ghosting gently when three small outboard-powered fishing boats approached. Six men. The first to reach us boldly asked for food. A moment of tense silence. "No, we need all we have," said Dan. They went away. We didn't have a gun. We had talked about bringing one, and this debate among sailors who sail farther offshore than Long Island Sound resembles the defend-or-submit choices of the pedestrian muggee. We both had the Keystone Cops idea of shouting down the hatch, "Max, wake up John and ask if we can spare something," or else running below and putting on sunglasses and a different hat and just eyeing the approaching boats through the barely opened forward hatch, playing a third crewman. It was over and, as in the Kingston taxi, we didn't do anything stupid. But scary. Our second fright in four days, and neither about Cape Horn.

On the first morning of this passage, neither of us was feeling marvelous, particularly me. Some shore-caught virus, we solemnly agreed, but Dan was over it in an hour or two. Hateful business, seasickness. I can live with my share of it, after all these years, and can lie or sit and let my mind drift, knowing that I can do what I must do when needed, and that this state won't last forever. But to use

Dan's phrase, there are moments when I wish a giant eraser would come down from the sky and quietly smudge me out. I also have learned that nervousness and fear help create seasickness, and that terror can instantly cure it. Also, these Vertues are not easy on the stomach, a trade-off for some of their fine qualities. The deep pendulum of the keel, containing almost 50 percent of the craft's total weight in the lead blob at its bottom, swings her more crisply than a boat with a greater proportion of weight higher up.

And then we started to move—the breeze built, and she lifted and started to fly south, close reaching in moderate seas. In one day we put back 153 miles, faster (in theory) than the little hull could move. But how beautifully she did move! In this little package there is all the strength and grace of *Rose of York*, the fine wooden thirty-eight-foot cutter, also designed by Laurent Giles, that I owned from 1963 to 1970, which carried us swiftly and comfortably from Falmouth, England, down to the Canary Islands and across to New York. All of Giles's genius is in this little hull that rises so lightly and falls so gently, surges ahead so powerfully, and steers with the steadiness of a long-keeled hull twice her length. On any craft that Giles himself drew, one feels the touch of a fine artist: what was new plus all that could be taken from wholesome tradition. He was a pioneer in creating light-displacement hulls (the fin-keeled anorexics I mentioned before), but under his hand they became ocean-going beauties, and even the reverse-sheer or humpbacked hulls were handsome. Little nineteen-foot *Sopranino* was sailed comfortably and quickly across the Atlantic by Patrick Ellam and Colin Mudie in 1952; *Myth of Malham* dominated British and Australian ocean racing in the late '40s and '50s; and *Samuel Pepys* and *Gulvain* should be noted for their pioneering designs: deck-stepped masts, the now prevalent reverse transom, the doghouse, backstay levers, on and on. Giles died in 1969.

After seeing hull #005 in Portsmouth, Dan and I drove to the famous offices in a Queen Anne house on a cobbled street in Lymington, and were handsomely shown about by Dick Stower, a partner. I knew much about Giles from Humphrey "Hum" Barton, who sailed one of the Vertues, *Vertue XXXV*, from England to New York in 1950, one of the first east–west small-boat crossings. Riding with a sea anchor in a hurricane off Bermuda, *Vertue XXXV* was thrown flat, and her impact on the water split the seam between her deck and cabin, letting in a lot of ocean. Perhaps the sea anchor was a mistake, Hum advised me; it held her against the wave. Hum was a brilliant seafarer and I was privileged to sail with him on his *Rose of York* before I bought her. Watching Hum in the cockpit was like watching a champion play squash—he was tall and spidery and seemed to have everything within easy reach. He was no youngster, but like an old actor, the years dropped away when he stood on his center stage.

I thought of this watching him jibe, a maneuver he preferred to "coming about," particularly in rough water: "Far less strain on the gear than all that shaking about when you're up into it," he said. With the tiller secured between his scrawny buttocks, he reached and let fly one set of running backstays with one hand, pulled down and set the lever of the windward-to-be runners with the other, and with the third hand (don't ask, I still haven't figured it out), he was reeling in the main sheet with such sinuous speed that the eye could not follow, and *overshecame*, with a gentle, "Care to the cranium, dear boy," at just the right millisecond as the boom swung over. And there she was, at full spread on the other tack, her lines so gently snubbed that you would know the jibe from only the change of heel if you hadn't seen it. Or, as I've said, almost seen it.

Dan and I learned to jibe *Sparrow* almost as well, but she has a simpler rig, without running backstays. No one's perfect—once I jibed by error in a tumultuous chop just as a friend was gently spilling flowers and her late husband's ashes into Vineyard Sound, and we spent a hilarious five minutes spitting them out and rubbing our eyes.

Hum was also a bit of a rascal, and when *Rose*'s engine quit, I discovered a crack in the head block, which we might have caused ourselves but for the mysterious application to the crack of a metal putty, covered by a new coat of British paint. I still liked Hum, and he didn't lose all of his fatherly affection for me when we met the next year and, under duress, he handed over almost enough cash to pay for the new engine. Hum had been Giles's partner, and his hands-on experience was valued. He told me that Giles didn't sail much because he was subject to seasickness.

"Do you think we can call this our Yom Kippur fast, Dad? I mean, does it count if you can't eat anyway?"

Dan and I started our watch-keeping, and he began to teach me the boat. The careful planning was successful, but it's never as simple as that, and Dan's time on board had revealed the subtle movements that save time and energy. He was patient: "Dad, you'll find it works better (faster, more securely in the dark) if you take the turn with your hand this way. Brace your feet like this . . ." It was so much his ship now, and that's what I'd hoped for. Contented, I tried not to be awkward and not to contradict, and was about 40 percent successful. This had been in my mind, and now it was clear: Dan would be captain. He'd put in more sailing time than I had over these last years, often solo. But the change was in our relationship, not in our abilities. It's natural; it comes with time. And thus the old saw: "When a father helps a son, both laugh—when a son helps a father, both cry." But it could be a no-lose situation for me. He would succeed and surpass because he had a great teacher.

Time usually heals seasickness, and in our cases, once it left us, it never visited again until after we'd set out from the next port. Most hateful for us both was that, being seasick, we couldn't read and be taken by words to another place. That, to me at least, is the nastiest trick of this malaise—the eye–stomach connection. Dan also added that he hated the indecision of its onset, an indecision of aim when you knew that both ends would discharge at once.

After two days and only one hundred slow miles out, I was well enough to read. We have a small aircraft chart light with a swing-in red filter to save night vision. Dan had rigged an exterior clip for this, high on the back of the dog-house (cabin house), and we could curl up there, snug under the canvas cockpit dodger during night watches. I had catching up to do, and started reading Dan's journals with his permission, learning of his adventures in *Sparrow* from Bastille Day in New London to Hangover Day in Port Royal.

DAN'S JOURNAL

New London to Swansboro

DAY 1. July 14. In sailing, you begin a voyage when you let go the lines holding you to land and surrender to the environment of water. As *Sparrow* sails slowly away from the dock, I am held just a bit longer—the eyes of friends and family follow me with ties of another sort, the real ones. When *Sparrow* is in the middle of the Thames River and my friends are small blurry dots, I begin at last to clear my mind and look about.

Sparrow is an English sloop designed for open sea and heavy weather, a type usually thought of as obsolete in today's rat race of faster boats. Dad and I bought the fiber-glass hull and have now spent two years of weekends, vacations, hours before breakfast, and any other fillable time slot completing her. I am thinking of this as I realize that the oozing sensation between the toes on my right foot is "5200," a viciously sticky silicone sealant that, when dry,

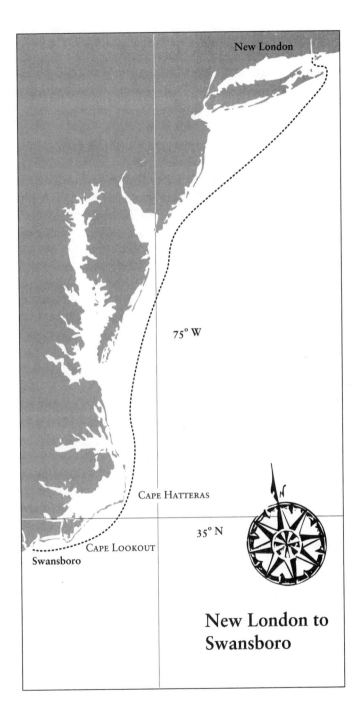

New London

75° W

Cape Hatteras

35° N

Cape Lookout

Swansboro

N

New London to
Swansboro

will waterproof the last bolt I installed just two hours ago. It takes a full day to dry, so I have twenty-two hours to find and clean each of the little footprints that are leading everywhere.

We're sailing by my home—the house my father and I built eight years ago on two-thirds of an acre of rock island at the mouth of the Thames River. We have a small motor launch to take us to our dock in the shallow, sheltered harbor behind the house. There we become cut off from land hassles—no phone, electricity, or unwanted company. The house is all wood, weathered, and rock-colored. We describe its style as "Japanese Victorian." My room is a tower on the third level. In it are my favorite books, hundreds of rocks, bones, and pieces of wood I've collected—each full of a memory. The room is very safe, and in it I am peaceful. I will miss this small place on Hobb's Island more than anything else.

Just as we were leaving, my friend Laine handed me an orange-and-white boy kitten. Into someone's video camera I sputtered the first name that came to mind, "Tiger," planted in my subconscious by endless episodes of "The Brady Bunch." He's hiding below, forward in the chain locker, and throwing up all over himself. Dad and I had talked about a ship's cat. He was more enthusiastic than I was. He thought it would help take our attention from our own problems and give us someone to talk to if we weren't talking to each other. I was worried about having something depending on me but was instantly pleased with this sweet little bit of fur.

Glenn, my crew, a never-before-been-on-a-boat-New-York-City-soon-to-be-famous playwright friend, has brought a gift: a full gallon of after-bath lotion. Now he battles a small kerosene fire on the untested stove. Black smoke billows out of the hatch. We're on our way.

The wind is blowing gently from the southwest, and I'm

grateful for this good weather. My father and I have sailed *Sparrow* for fewer than five hours in this harbor. The boat is 95 percent done—ready for her first voyage. Dad can't join me for two months, so my job is to get *Sparrow* to Jamaica, where he'll come aboard. This first shake-up (or -down) cruise will be to Florida. Maybe it's dumb to take a boat offshore for her first sail, but then again, how else will we learn what's not ready? We change course toward West Harbor, on the inside of Fishers Island. We need a night to acclimatize ourselves to the ship. We anchor over a sandy bottom in eighteen feet of water and almost instantly fall asleep. We have been through two solid days of last-minute chaos and need to rest, separated from land. Here we'll put charts away, stow food, and get ready to become an independent unit with water all around us.

DAY 2. Up early. I am conscious that we have a great secret on board. This small sailboat is preparing for the Roaring Forties and Cape Horn. We don't need a terrified family. They believe we will pass through the Strait of Magellan, which (they don't know this) is actually worse.

Glenn makes a terrific breakfast—he is up on the latest New York diets and cooks food like a chef; I've made a good choice bringing him on board. He is blond, small, muscly, and very gentle. I don't need any ego-threatening here—I've enough when relaxed in a bathtub—and Glenn projects peace. He also can sit down and tell you what your feelings are doing, making me feel like I've been out to lunch on myself. He's come sailing, completely out of his element, to discover "all new material."

Hundreds of details all day. I teach Glenn how to whip a line—a fancy sewing trick sailors have so the end of a rope doesn't unravel. He does about fifty of them, and my fingers burn from pinching the ends of the Dacron line, which I've melted to be doubly sure the ends stay together. After dinner we swim, making ourselves seem angels of glow light with the phosphorescent creatures—water fireflies—that our arms and legs disturb. Glenn lives for aesthetically pleasing moments like this and he seems to be purring happiness.

We sit on deck and look north to the home lights that have guided my family's sailing and fishing for almost as long as I can remember, up to Burr's Yacht Haven or to our Hobb's Island house. This is a beautiful place, perfect to come home to. From our house, or just a few feet south by outboard down our front lawn of water, you can see or hear nine big marks. First there's New London Harbor Light, old but not much help; we call it "Old B.V." (Barely Visible). New London Ledge marks the river mouth right in the middle of the channel; it's exactly one mile south of Hobb's Island. At the mouth of Fishers Island Sound is North Dumpling, and ten miles east is Latimer Reef, a good-looking striped lighthouse. Then Watch Hill, Rhode Island. We see Montauk's big bang of a flash, eighteen miles south, on the tip of Long Island. In the Sound is Bartlett's Reef, just a metal tower but with a sharp-sounding horn. At the tip of Long Island's north fork, there is the Plum Island light with its quick spark, and east of that is Little Gull, a rare steady (not flashing) light. Race Rock, around which we fish, looks like a Bavarian castle, and we will round that when we go to sea. The waters here are swift and can challenge you with currents that are fast enough to brush up a steep chop when the wind blows in the opposite direction, like stroking a cat's fur the wrong way.

The Thames is a thirty-mile-long estuary, fresh at its north end and salt for the last eight miles where it flows past the submarine base, chemical factories, and cities of New London and Groton. Every time someone bulldozes near the shore they find remains of Native American settlements, and I'm usually embarrassed to see what's happening on those shores. At times I long to forget.

We pronounce the river's name "*Th*ames," with the "th" like "thistle," instead of the British "tems." The reason, Dad says, is because the British always pronounced it the way it is spelled—they're not stupid, he likes to add— until George the First came to the throne (trone?) from Hanover, and he couldn't pronounce "th." The King's English didn't mean good English, but rather the way the King said things, and so everybody had to say it his way. But our river was named before George the First ascended. There's a little town along the English river called Thame and still pronounced the old way, because the King never happened to mention it. Dad likes to lie in wait for people who are embarrassed about our hick pronunciation, then he pounces on them with this blurt of intellectualism . . .

DAY 3. Wearing full yellow battle gear, we set sail at 1400 hours. The water in The Race is rough, the current is fast. We take this new seasick medicine—it's a plastic, nickel-sized patch you stick on behind your ear. Glenn gets sleepy and I get depressed—both are known side effects of this medicine. Apparently, some people even hallucinate from the stuff.

And now as I write, I am also very seasick. Night descends, with fog, and that depresses me. The compass has a twelve-degree error—twelve degrees! It's been years since I've done any navigation, and between the current, thick night, and dense fog, we are quite lost and this also depresses me. Glenn and the cat are not sick, and I'm even more depressed about that. Wearing half of lunch, I adjust the never-fully-tested automatic steering gear—a wind vane made by Navik—and head us toward where I hope deep water is. I sleep in the cockpit, mildewing in my foul-weather gear as rain sneaks in the sleeves and down my neck. I wake every half-hour but am too depressed to go below to check the charts and figure out which lighthouse we've just passed. The violent motion of *Sparrow* climbing steep waves and the kerosene smell make these visits at least twenty seconds too short—pencils can't make X's on puke-covered charts. So I never really get our position. Glenn and the cat are asleep in a cuddleknot. We are wearing storm sails already—eight-foot seas in a strong south-southwesterly wind. What the hell am I doing here?

DAY 4. Meals appear (after many one-sided discussions between Glenn and the Deity regarding the latter's policy of rocking the boat) with a wisp of watercress or a thin slice of lemon. The cat now knows how to use his litter box, but manages even when having all four legs in it to place the important end outside, so he's confused when we yell at him.

DAY 5. Our world consists of angles. When the boat's heeled over, getting a pen from where it's lodged itself can be a major job. One moment it's calm, and the next, every bit of energy is needed to scrape down a sail and haul up another one. The weather becomes a feared god, and all I have are muscles and tenacity. Each day I spend hours calculating where the dot I call *me* belongs on the chart. The barometer is rising as I write and the cat's passed out in his water dish—it's very hot. Since the wind is naturally dead against us, we zig offshore for maybe forty miles, then zag back toward land till we see a lighthouse, maybe even recognizing it from the chart (this happens rarely, I do confess).

I'd like to be home balled up on the couch watching a movie about this and eating Chinese food.

DAY 7. Last night I lay on deck listening to how big the ocean is. We are expecting an Ocean City landfall. This is unimpressive progress passing New Jersey. Glenn changes sails all "frothy at the mouth," which I think means "with terror." Being a playwright, he's a bit elegant for this and very dramatic. He strolls around (as much as one can "stroll" on a twenty-five-foot boat) in his black silk kimono.

We tow a can of gazpacho to cool for supper and he complains my fondue forks are rusty. He scolds me when I wipe my mouth with the cat.

"Hey, Dan, do we have any sour cream?"

"Sure, Glenn, by the 10/24 half-inch stainless flatheads, under the starboard quarter berth."

"What the hell is all that?"

"I dunno, I just made it up."

"You mean we don't have sour cream?"

Fishing boats from New Jersey head east in the early morning and west in the evening. Last night we came close to some commercial boats dragging deep nets. I shined the spotlight on our sails to let them see us. In the morning I sailed right up to a floating plastic-mesh bucket with barnacles growing on it. I pulled it on board and it now holds three hundred feet of our port anchor line, and neatens the fo'c'sle a bit.

DAY 8. I've taken the brave first step back into the world of celestial navigation. Two sextant sun shots today; both put us in the Atlantic, plus or minus a small continent. It takes a while to remember which numbers you add or subtract to other numbers.

DAY 10. Past Delaware and Virginia, north of Cape Hatteras, we are lulled all day by the genoa pulling us. The "genny" is our largest working sail. She's big and can only stay up in fairly light wind, but she can really pull you along, because if the wind is that gentle, so is the sea, and the waves don't stop you. A light breeze by night as we move along a brightly lit shore. Lots of landmarks tell me our position.

The rigging on board is simple. The mainsail has four reefs, meaning that there are four settings besides full up. We can haul the sail down to reach them in succession as the wind picks up. The first reef is for winds over about fifteen knots (nautical miles per hour). We have a system for remembering which color-coded line to haul to bring the sail down to one of its smaller sizes. Red for the first reef stands for "mere general fear." If it blows over twenty, one turns green with nauseating terror, and one secures the green line, which is the second reef. Next it's blowing over thirty knots and shock has set in (the blood has left your extremities), and you pull the blue line for the third reef. If the wind picks up more than that, you're scared to death. White is appropriate. That makes the sail tiny. This mnemonic system makes sailing simple and allows us to concentrate fully on our anxiety.

Some of my earliest memories are on board our family's first boat, a thirty-eight-foot wooden cutter, *Rose of York,* a larger version of *Sparrow.* Dad sailed her from England to New York, and I remember the smell of her when I was just three. Dad and I wanted a cutter rig on *Sparrow,* so we put on a foresail. This small sail, only fifteen square feet, which is about as big as a beach towel, serves three important functions. First and most important, its stay is a great thing to grab just before you get washed over. Second, the tiny sail with its own boom can be pushed to catch wind on the "wrong" side when you bring up your anchor, thus giving you some leverage to maneuver the engineless boat in a crowded harbor. Third, when "heaving to" ("stalling" is a better word—keeping the boat riding easily in bad weather), you lash it to the side opposite the reefed main, and the boat is confused and just sits in place.

MIDNIGHT. We relax as a light breeze carries us along the brightly lit shore. We eat some popcorn and have a shot of rum. I take the first morning watch and think of climbing trees.

I fall asleep on deck for a couple of hours. I wake as *Sparrow* lifts and a loud roar—not from any direction but all around—fills my ears. I jerk up and see a beach and house looming directly ahead. Waves are breaking *on the beach* only fifty yards from *Sparrow*'s bow! I yank off the self-steerer and turn her hard toward deeper water. We are moving well, and she puts her nose to the wind. There is that pause that boats have, that moment when the sails flap, uncertain which way to go. Glenn has run on deck and is crouched by the compass. Thumps—we are dropped twice on sand by a big wave—then ever so slowly we pick up speed as if it had all been a stunt to impress someone, and we sail away on the next tack.

Glenn tries to help: "How about them Mets, huh?"

My mind is in overdrive, and I can hardly believe we are in deep water again. I envision *Sparrow* as she would have been: lying on her side, waves and sand crashing on us. My home, on a beach.

> BOY WRECKS FATHER'S YACHT ON CALM NIGHT,
> DRINKING SUSPECTED.

Then eight minutes later, at 0210, a Coast Guard cutter zips up and asks if we've shot off or seen any flares. Strange. It's like I've just gone back in time, rearranged the past, and woken up five seconds earlier to prevent what would have happened. Five feet or five seconds would have been it. I feel twilight-zoned.

Now we're booming along at five knots toward Hatteras—red strokes of clouds all over and a lot of wind, with the starboard rail under water. Cape Hatteras is where the Gulf Stream, a strong north-bound current, bounces off the U.S. coast and heads out to England. The warm water causes local clouds that often rain on the beach. The current tears up the ocean floor, constantly changing its depths.

DAY 11. Tiger is making toilet paper confetti out of the fifty feet he's treadmilled off the roll.

Slow progress. Needless to say, when wind, waves—

whatever—are seemingly "against" you here at sea, they become Living Entities and are treated as such. The chart shows Diamond Shoal as a twenty-mile shallow area, and it can't be more specific because the bottom changes by the hour. We have up the small red jib and the main reefed once. We're crawling. It's clear to me that we'll never get by unless we go over the shoal close to land where the current is less strong. Hatteras will do this to sailing ships: it will make them take risks.

Glenn stands forward with the lead line—a weight on a cord with knots every six feet. He tosses the weight ahead of *Sparrow* and hauls it tight as it hits bottom, just as we sail over that spot. He counts the knots and calls back the depth. We need at least five feet of water, which leaves us just six inches of clearance when it's calm. Here the waves are steep and fixed over certain places. *Sparrow* slides sideways at them, never seeming to gain any way. Finally I think screw it, we'll just go through one and hope for the best. My heart is pounding. You can't be sure there isn't a rocky ledge underneath. Glenn calls, "Fifteen—twelve—nineteen—*seven*." My heart misses a beat. But we're over the shoal. A wave hits us and water cascades along the deck and out the scuppers. The striped lighthouse is beautiful behind us. There are Jeeps scattered along the beach and lots of muscly guys drinking beer in the sun with their bikini babes. If we'd wrecked on the beach, we'd have gotten a beer and a ride into town from people who looked like they had stepped off the cover of *Esquire*.

Glenn says I have a sweet tooth for psychologically dangerous situations, the kind that make me feel invincibly alone. I sit back and wonder that I should be worth knowing.

DAY 12. Becalmed almost all day, we hear loud booms from the northeast, like Civil War cannons. Hundreds of two-inch fish jump in unison all around us. Afterward dark, strange, "close encounters of the third kind" lights are visible on the shore, later determined to be dirt bikers playing in the sand dunes.

DAY 13. Frustrating night with totally no wind interrupted by several violent half-hour squalls. At 0500 I am so pissed I just drop anchor off the beach, let out all the chain, and we sleep for a few hours with barely a ripple to distinguish *Sparrow* from a motel room. At 0900, the wind comes up from the southwest and we interrupt our first *not moving* breakfast, jump over for a splash, and then set sail. I take an accurate noon sight—so nice to get familiar with the sextant again! Then I take a late-afternoon sight that I find to be 1,206.8 nautical miles off, and I am unable to locate the error.

It's a stormy night rounding Cape Lookout. (You think Cape Lookout is a bad name—the next one is Cape Fear.) We lose the lid to the rice pot and a knife over the side while doing dishes—both stainless steel and doomed to eternity.

After dinner Glenn reads some Edgar Allan Poe out loud. The Navik is working well, steering us accurately and giving us time to relax. The sky is dark and lightning flashes, throwing spooky shadows on us.

DAY 14. Exhausted from hours rounding Cape Lookout, I see the dawn with my red eyes. Glenn's "Cape Lookout Banana Pudding," like a vampire, couldn't handle the sunrise, so I throw the remains of it overboard as he sleeps. The wind picks up and by 1000, *Sparrow* is churning along the coast off North Carolina. The seas are steep and the motion is violent. We decide to go into Bogue Inlet. It doesn't look bad on the chart.

Sailing in under the third reef and the second jib, we suddenly are committed to this little opening in the shoreline with twenty-five knots of wind dead astern and surf on either side. It's an awful feeling on a sailboat, and there's no choice anymore. We seem to be moving fast—yes, the current is strong and with us. We'll have less time to figure out which way to go. We'll have to start our turning early. A sharp right, a left, and then the feel of sand grinding under our keel. Swishing sounds. We're stuck on a sandbar and the current whirls around us. Glenn looks at me. I'm sure I've turned white. My skin is clammy. It's so pretty out! Clean sky and girls in bright bikinis almost within reach. I swallow and casually say, "Tide's coming in, we'll get off in a minute," and my voice cracks only a little. Suddenly, spinning us around, the current does free us, and we have a fast quarter-mile to Casper's Marina, where we anchor. *Sparrow* is pinned back by the strong current, completely motionless, the anchor chain taut like those you see welded into mailbox posts.

"Hurry up, Glenn, let's get ashore!"

"OK, OK, let me get my purse."

"Purse? Glenn, we're in North Carolina! Call it an ammunition pouch or something."

We make a few phone calls, revise a few schedules, and Glenn is off to the airport. I'll continue alone down the coast. Next stop is Charleston, about two hundred miles, to pick up my next crew. At sea, I'm untangled and am in charge of my universe. On land, there's a web that catches my every movement and sends out many vibrations. Yet once afloat, I'm free, whereas Glenn can't be. He is caught and tugged by the schedules of land life. I couldn't possibly hold him. He's going to have his first play produced soon and is all bubbles about it.

DAY 16. I'm aground again in the same place. I have this fear an airplane will fly over and take pictures to be made into "Swansboro, North Carolina," postcards and right smack dab in the middle will be *Sparrow* on her side.

A blue crab looks up at me looking down at him. He's pissed I'm moving his sandbar. I'm tempted to get out the net and eat him, but decide I'd rather he go on with his life. Tiger falls into the toilet and emerges on deck looking like a tangled coat hanger.

The Coast Guard tows me out. As their engines fade back into the inlet—back in toward the land of restaurants, wives, warm beds, and bathtubs—it grows still. I raise sail and put off, south. I'm scared of getting seasick, scared of too much wind, and scared of being alone.

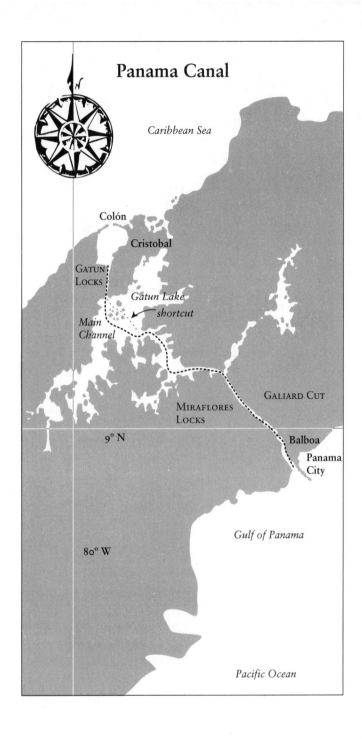

Panama Canal

Caribbean Sea

Colón

Cristobal

GATUN
LOCKS

Gatun Lake
shortcut

*Main
Channel*

MIRAFLORES
LOCKS

GALIARD CUT

Balboa

Panama
City

9° N

80° W

Gulf of Panama

Pacific Ocean

4 PANAMA

*If Cape Horn is to be seen only once, this is
how it should be seen, with islands and dark
sounds behind it, the very tip of that great
continent. To see it in sunshine would be out
of character; . . . From False Cape Horn
ahead to Deceit Island now behind, like the
half-submerged backbone of some monstrous
skeleton, all was clear, cold, and grey.*

   —Miles Smeeton, Because the Horn Is There

DAVID

By landfall, along the Panama coast, the wind was
gone. Dan aimed a touch down the coast in the old tradition of being sure which way to turn when land came up,
but perhaps that was unnecessary with such a dazzling
target as the canal entrance. Add a few miles error. I was
annoyed with Dan.

"Dammit, Dad, if I spend all my time trying to find my
mistakes, I won't have time to make new ones."

There was no wind, and we were shut out as if a gate
closed. We spent three days creeping the last few miles to
Panama. I yanked off the lines to the self-steerer: "I can do
better than this thing." I couldn't. It was beautiful, despite
the heat. Approaching Cristobal, there are small islands
that shoot up like Enoshima, near Tokyo—a Japanese
mist-broken landscape. Our last night was spent passing
an anchored freighter in the enveloping, hypnotizing, deep
thrum of her generators. Four hundred feet in six hours.

I was tired in the morning, still sunburned, my ass hurt
from a fall on the compass box, and after a snide remark

from Dan about my impatience—and I cannot remember it—I had a fit and threw a shirt overboard. This instantly brought up a breeze, and we were in, past the great break-water, and directed to one of the yacht anchorage areas. A giant steel launch surged up and we were inspected. Dan showed me how to disconnect the Navik gear without losing the bolts overboard—again.

It had been our first voyage together on *Sparrow*. So-so for me—my excitement blurred by discomforts, seasickness, and burns—but we were there, and we did it! No, *Sparrow* did it! And now, a new town.

"Ahoy, *Sparrow*," called a burly man in a rubber boat with an outboard. "I'm going in. Welcome." He was a live-aboard, one of the thousands who laze or work from port to port in yachts big or small, elegant or in shambles. He pointed out his modern sailboat, about forty-two feet, already encrusted with rusting windmill generators, a scooter, and window boxes. "Can't really feel the sea, like a big boat, unless you're forty feet." He showed us through Cristobal. Always was a nasty town, he said, and now out of control, since the Americans left. He showed us the whorehouse, the hardware shop, and a few other notable spots, but his monologue was so steeped in ugly racial terms that we shortened the tour. He took us to the local boat club, which was wrapped around a Chinese restaurant. There was a slip open. He rowed us out and we sailed *Sparrow* in. Dan gave me this responsibility—he must have felt that I was better at bringing a boat into a dock under sail. Or he wanted to stand aside for skills I was proud of. Of course, he couldn't just stand by—"Now, Dad. Now!" Well, we compromised, she made it. God, it was hot.

We survived a week of awful Spanish-Chinese food and junky cold drinks. Cristobal is a rusty town. We would cross a vast container yard to reach a few airy colonial-style buildings used by officials at this end of the canal—some tropical plantings, some raggy lawns, general disrepair.

Then the town started beyond the rail terminal—cheap shops with cheap dry goods, video stores, street stands, garages, machine shops, crowds of shoppers, and even more standers-by. Some gave us well-meant warnings: "Don't go into that street, plenty robbers." If there were buildings of any grace, they were hidden behind peeling signs and billboards. There were a few broad avenues with central strips that might once have had grass. It was crowded, but no one seemed at home; the people could have been an occupying force. If the blare of music from the shops and strolling boomboxes suddenly stopped, one could imagine the whole population moving one house down or one hallway up, like musical chairs, with no one noticing the difference.

In a curious way, this place seemed all port and no town, a pit stop with rootless inhabitants, and we didn't desire to see, enjoy, or try to understand it. I ragged Dan about being behind schedule, but we went over the calendar and he calmed me. "We want to be off The Horn before the end of January," he said. "Twelve weeks. We're fine." After the days of awful heat, terrible food, and countless little tasks, we took our showers and tried to relax after a deep-fried meal. I started reading Dan's journals again. Why the hell had he put himself through that slow and cranky slog down the coast, with foul wind, foul current, all the predictable Hatteras angst?

"You should have headed straight out for Bermuda, cutting through the Gulf Stream south of Montauk, then from Bermuda right down to the Bahamas and the Windward Passage. You could have reached out and then come in on the westerlies."

"Dad, Glenn couldn't have stayed."

"Sure he could. He stayed two weeks, and it's only seven hundred miles or so to Bermuda; that allows just sixty per day. You put back an average of eighty on that awful poke to Swansboro."

"What if something went wrong?"

"It did."

"I mean basic rigging, pumps, seacocks."

"We should have jammed her out to sea for three hard days. Would have saved time in the long run, and misery too."

"Couldn't have picked up my next crews."

"Betcha John would have flown out to Hamilton or, hell, rowed out. He's tough."

"What about my navigation?"

"You can hit Bermuda on the radio beacon and a noon line—simple stuff."

"Well, Dad, what about Carol?" No response. "Dad, I guess I preferred to improvise along shore, and not commit. Okay, you win. I'll give it a seven on the hindsight scale."

And then we both said, "Hold it! Hurricane season! Down to a two on the hindsight scale."

I remembered a bad cruise to Bermuda on the *Rose of York* with my brother and a married couple. Bad starting weather, and Betty snuggled into her berth, justifiably terrified, for four days. We wanted to celebrate Passover, and she had brought the necessary foods, but on the first night she was finally able to crawl on deck all we could manage was to eat warm peas from bowls with spoons. There is a tradition of opening the door for the prophet Elijah during the Seder. I went to open the forward hatch for him, and suddenly three dolphins leaped together, thirty feet from the boat, high and clean out of the water. We hadn't seen them approach and didn't see them arch up for breath again. It was miraculous. "Elijah," Betty said. My ancestors had to wait for God to part the seas, and now we sailed over them on a yacht.

The weather wasn't the only unpleasant part of that cruise. My brother had a powerful older-brother hold on me, and for the only time in my life I lost the confidence of command. *Rose*'s bilge was sealed in the British tradition, with her wooden ribs leveled up with tar, so bilge water wouldn't be trapped between them. But a five-gallon kerosene tank rusted through, dissolving the tar. So we were a filthy, sticky black mess below, and I had a tantrum about that. Then I unwrapped my celestial almanac, which had arrived by mail the day we left, and it was the wrong one, not starting for two weeks. Extrapolating the numerical tables backward was tedious, not difficult, but my brother had a blast of anger about that. Finally, there was his schedule. He had to be back on a certain day, and the tension grew. That's when I learned never to permit tight shore timetables on a boat. I sympathized with Dan on that. Yet I remember a beautiful sunset over pearl water and lavender air when we all sat in the cockpit and read to each other from Conrad's *The Mirror of the Sea*. I accepted my brother's annoyance, but he kept muttering that I didn't know where we were and I'd never find the island, and that wore me down. On the morning of my predicted landfall, I came on deck at first light. My brother was at the tiller. Less than a mile to leeward was the *Queen of Bermuda*, exactly parallel to us, harbor bound and dead slow. In her wake, a mile astern, was the *Empress of Bermuda*, dead slow. "Well, shit, they're lost too," I said, and somehow this irritated my brother.

Now the table was certainly turned. Off Panama, I was grumbling about Dan's navigation, and it was his sassy remark that blew me up.

DAN'S JOURNAL

Swansboro to Hawksbill Cay
DAY 17

Dear Max and Michelle,
   Tiger and I are between Cape Fear and Charleston, S.C. It's gray all around. My first north wind is

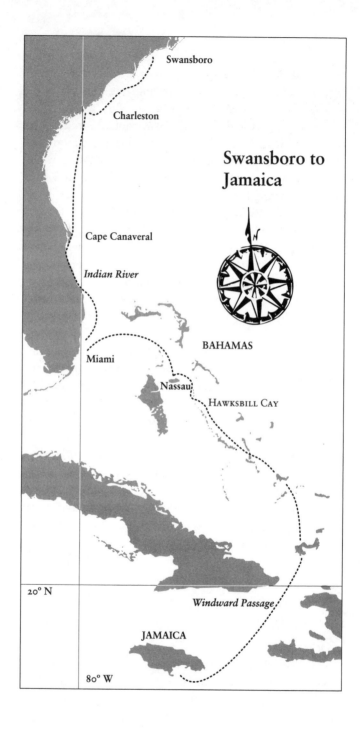

Swansboro

Charleston

Swansboro to Jamaica

Cape Canaveral

Indian River

BAHAMAS

Miami

Nassau

HAWKSBILL CAY

20° N

Windward Passage

JAMAICA

80° W

blowing, which means I sail downwind and in the right direction, rather than beating against it in zags. There are four-foot seas following me and we surf or skitter down the fronts of them. Night is scary.

The self-steering keeps me on course relative to the wind, not to the compass, so if the wind changes so does our direction. This is our "Navik." It's a cool combination of a windmill, a sundial, and an extra pair of hands. There is the wind part, a vane, that you rotate with a knob that fixes it so that its narrow edge faces into the wind at whatever angle the wind is to the ship. When the boat goes off course—relative to the wind—the wind vane is blown flat. This is a more positive and stronger move than if it just swiveled. When it is flat, or almost flat, it yanks up a rod that turns a little rudder at the back of a paddle that is down in the water trailing *Sparrow*. That little rudder deflects the paddle sideways, against the water flowing by it, so it is swept up, and that's a powerful move because it now lies flat-side to the moving water, and it pulls lines that pull the main tiller of *Sparrow,* which of course turns *Sparrow*'s rudder until she is back on course, and then the vane and the paddle become thin-edged to the wind and water again, and we are on course.

I guess you have to be there, and there isn't really a sundial. What you have to do is balance the boat perfectly anyway, with the right sails on, well trimmed, so the Navik nudges it to stay where it really wants to be, instead of forcing it to be somewhere else.

You fuss with the sails and tweak the knob and adjust the lines that go to the tiller and all of that takes patience and is harder than just steering but you do it once or twice an hour for a couple of minutes and then Navik takes the job off your hands for the rest of the time. In steady wind and sea conditions you may not have to touch it for days at a time.

Sometimes I wake from suffocating dreams to find Tiger purring happily on my face and I'm breathing fur. His meow has improved a little. If you squeeze him you can hear it.

Like you, Max, I thrive on audience and here, alone, I do imagine one, but ultimately have none. There isn't the slightest trace of the thrilling possibility that someone is watching me. And I'm glad. I'd far rather do and be than always wonder how I look. I'm at my best when I know that no one watches me.

I'm behind schedule and anxious. I want to get everything built in Florida on time. The list of jobs has tripled since we left. There's lots of details left. The sun didn't set tonight, it just grayed out. In fact, everything is graying out and the sea looks like mercury. I have the #1 jib on, which means I can sleep easier—it can stay up in a lot of wind. Thunderstorms always seem to have evil intent when you sail. They find you. Then I see beauty in the turmoil and all goes well . . . Love, Dan

Tiger is on his morning "spaz run." It begins when he sits bolt upright from a sound sleep and leaps eight inches straight up. Because the boat is rocking, he lands four inches to the left and thus assumes he is under assault. He sprints over the wet-gear locker into the quarter berth and frantically scratches a roll of sailcloth. Next he tiptoes back along the handrail, falling into the basket of fruit and attacking an orange. He then springs out like a Ping-Pong ball and attacks the entire toilet, a bite on the rim and a paw at the hose. Next a pen rolling on the floor is investigated with attack eyes, then during his cat leap at the pen, a fly buzzes by catching his attention and he crashes into the bulkhead, his eyes following the fly. Then that look that only cats have, the look that says, "What fly? I did that on purpose."

DAY 18. 0300. I check the horizon and am impressed with how clear it is. The lights from some town flicker out as *Sparrow* sails through the trough of a wave, reappearing as she bobs over the top.

0430. Our motion changes—I'm halfway on deck before I've even opened my eyes, and when I stagger through the hatch I wish they were still closed. All around me are patches of surf, and those lights over the horizon are street lamps just beyond the sand dunes directly ahead.

I'm naked, the cold rain is pelting my back—it's so stormy the lampposts disappear as visibility is reduced to the closest whitecaps only. We are booming along at five knots straight downwind. The whisker pole is set, holding our small spinnaker. The wind had shifted and, I realize, my wrist alarm did not buzz.

The next three hours take about four days. All the lines are tangled, all thirteen feet of the whisker pole swings at me, sails drag through the water. I fall twice. I am filled with a pulsing anticipation of the moment we will hit the beach or some rocky outcrop. I cannot see the land and I do not know where I am on the chart.

All I can do is scramble and claw through the chaos. Although messy, after a while I have things under control. Well, control is perhaps the wrong word because I still don't know where it might be better to be. All around are whitecaps—surf on rocks, I am sure—and visibility is maybe two hundred feet. I sail back and forth, straining to see through the black, for hours. Sunrise is at least two hours late, and when it happens, I feel saved. I can see the land—I have sailed into a bay and have been tacking back and forth in the middle. I ease the sheet and reset the Navik, aiming for the larger blue.

I curse at the Navik, "Is that what you're gonna do, you rotten sonofabitch?" I sound like Dad, who thinks everything's alive, and tries to reason with things, thanks them or cusses them out.

DAY 19. South Carolina. After hours of windless heat, I reach Charleston at last. A stream of brown yuck oozes out between the narrow breakwaters—a clear line between sea and city—as if the ocean outside the breakwaters would not admit to being associated with the water within.

I've arrived, and in my own and nature's time. Sailing is just sailing, but being human we distort it into "getting somewhere." That's why I like not having a motor—I have to be resigned to dealing with what the ocean throws me.

DAY 20. August 2. I'm in Charleston to pick up John Coe, my crew to Florida. He meets me on the dock. John's in his fifties and looks exactly like one of those carved and painted Maine fisherman statues you can buy at a touristy gas station. Exactly. He knows about eight times as much about sailing as I do.

DAY 21. Good to be at sea again! John's already learned how everything works. He shows me a photograph of *Mistress Quickly*, a steel schooner he is building. I tease him on his fifth year of work, remembering a summer and another boat when he didn't finish applying the seventh coat of perfectly smooth varnish on his mast until it was time to put the boat up for the winter.

I first saw John when I was about eight, and Dad had to explain some of it later. We were on the dock in New London to make an evening visit. John is an actor and had a summer job in the area. He had sailed down from New York and was living on his boat, *Godot*, which was like a Lightning-class boat but bigger, about twenty feet long, no cabin, all cockpit for day sailing. John had stretched a tarpaulin over the boom and was living in that small tent.

Instead of calling out "Ahoy, *Godot*," or something like

that, Dad put a silencing finger to his lips. On board, we could see a warm glow from a kerosene lantern, and John sat by the little cabin table helping his cat give birth. I remember his Santa Claus–bearded face with its expression of joyfulness and wonder as he lifted each kitten. We watched for a while and then tiptoed away. The cat's name was You Damn Fool, which John "shortened" to You Damn Fool Cat, and he tells me now that she had a perky way of standing on the cockpit seat with her paws on the coaming and looking around. People would sail by and call out, "What's the cat's name?" and John would shout over, "You Damn Fool."

John also tells the best fog story. On that trip down to New London he sailed inside Faulkner Island, and suddenly dense fog set in. He cut his little outboard and drifted, waiting for the fog to lift, assuming he was out in the channel, hoping to hear other boats or a bell buoy. All was quiet, and for a long time. Suddenly a screen door slammed and someone called, "Here, kitty, kitty!"

Sailing with John is a huge success. We are at ease together and I have full confidence in his seamanship. Just as important, he has full confidence in me, which allows me to grow as a captain. We alternate three-hour watches, and with no worries when John's on watch, I catch up on sleep. The trip is uneventful except for great schools of dolphin. Through the fiberglass hull, which is a good sounding board, I can hear them chatting away. I also catch up on my navigation: radio fixes, good dead reckoning, current effect, sun sights, moon sights, Jupiter, Polaris. I recapture my old skills and I'm good. I learned coastal navigation over the years with Dad, and during my solo year on *Minitaur*. I learned celestial navigation in class on board the barkentine *Regina Maris*, on a two-month whale-counting cruise near Haiti five years ago.

I'm upset by the chart of this South Carolina and Georgia coast, which every few inches indicates unexploded mines, rocket casings, torpedoes, chemical warfare dumpings, and other things that I don't like being on top of.

Tiger is now big enough to jump up on deck and even get below again, but he prefers a lift. He looks up at you, scrunches his face like a blowfish and silently mouths "me-ow."

DAY 27. Becalmed above Cape Canaveral, but John knows just how to "scratch the mast" for wind, and soon we're in at Canaveral Cut and then sail *Sparrow* south on the Indian River to Eau Gallie where friends Peter and Katie Feller have a house and dock. For the last one hundred yards we're becalmed, and I wave at a guy in a passing speedboat and he gives us a tow. He casts off, and with just a little remaining momentum, *Sparrow* schlurps to a halt in the mud, three feet from her destination. We jump ashore, make a sort of rope catwalk, and immediately retreat as Chauncy, a 110-pound mastiff, runs at us. (Knowing the dog is friendly is part of the problem; he always has a huge goober hanging from his jowls, and it always, *always*, gets you in the face.) Peter and Katie hear the commotion and we are rescued. We take baths, and later in the day John gets on an airplane for home. Mullet are jumping. The water is calm, like a big puddle. I can hear them leave the water, flittering their tails in the air. Are they jumping to or from? Am I sailing to or from?

DAY 29. I drilled a small hole through the hull below the waterline today and I'm not in a good mood. Only after running into the house to gleefully call my dad did Peter return to hand me a cork to put in the hole in place of my finger.

DAY 38. It's been eight days now of Florida sweat. Day and night are indistinguishable, both full to bursting with measurements, compounds, varnishes, paints, wires, hoses, and fittings. Sleep is the same—in dreams I review the day's mistakes or anticipate tomorrow's confusions. I'm not as skillful as Dad with tools, but I do manage to fix a spice rack, put toggles and turnbuttons over all the compartments and drawers, and install the solar cells to keep our two twelve-volt batteries charged. I rig rainwater traps for the longer legs of the trip. *Sparrow* absorbs it all and with each refinement is more ready. Everything below that is not attached is encased. I drill small holes and pass parachute cord through to hold in objects and books, and to press them down. My theory is that *Sparrow* will be rolled over completely and since I hate mess, I don't want to clean up afterward as well as prevent her from sinking. Actually Dad and I disagree about messes. His is all over the house at home. I moralize at him, but my own room is a kind of disaster. But we agree about wanting to sink neatly.

Pete gives me two twelve-foot oars, and we can now row *Sparrow*. Tiger goes to a vet and gets poked everywhere; hundreds of fleas, bugs, mites, and worms are now homeless. The compass is adjusted by a local named "Terrible Tucker" who doesn't like ecologists but loves looking at my Valley girlfriend, a college friend who flies in. I'm excited for her company. Carol is very much from California—she ends all statements in a question—and has never been on a boat, ever. We took a dance class together and never entangled our friendship with sex (usually a necessary, or at least constant, puzzle for me). Carol is bubbly and fun to be around—eager to work (except when "General Hospital" is on)—and, well, after all this time it's nice to talk to someone in a bikini. She is high-energy, worships her BMW, and can cry on a dime. We go shopping in our last all-American supermarket and easily spend seven hundred dollars.

DAY 39. At sunset Pete and Katie tow us out of the little harbor and into the Indian River. We anchor and wave. *Sparrow* is once again free from the land. The bugs ignore me and go right to Carol. She's better than one of those electric, blue-light bug zappers. Forget *port* and *starboard*. Carol struggles with *right* and *left*, tangled in "all those string things," and is peeling off her first and second layers of skin, sunburnt crispy.

DAY 42. Sailing down the Indian River has been difficult— the channel is filled with little islands, man-made from dredged-up river bottom during the Depression. They now support bushes, pine trees, and bugs. This morning we swam to a little one, and I told Carol to look out for tarantulas, mud snakes, and banana spiders. She screamed. Swimming back to *Sparrow* I almost drowned—she was clinging to me in terror.

DAY 45. Anchored outside the Miami Harbor entrance, we awake to city noises and the wake of large passenger ships. I make a terrific spaghetti breakfast (Tiger *loved* it) and we spend much of the day recovering. We've come this far south because the Gulf Stream will carry us north as we cross it. We are waiting till 2100 to head out—toward the Bahamas—hoping to arrive in daylight. We listen to the weather forecast—to get caught in the Stream when the wind comes from the north is messy—very steep seas. Dad and I have sailed across the Stream from here in a nine-foot open sailing dinghy. It was a beautiful dinghy that Pete Feller made. It had come to New York as a prop in an English show (Pete is in theatre also) and was just half a boat, with "1879" carved on it. He made a mold and cast a few in fiberglass. This was during my *Minitaur* year—1980. For the dinghy's one-hundredth birthday, we sailed her from here to West End, on Grand Bahama Island, with *Minitaur* as the mother ship. After a slow start, the wind picked up, and the little boat seemed to jump forward off the steep short crests. We (Dad) dumped her over twice:

she didn't tip in but turned over backwards, to windward, in sudden holes in the wind. We righted her and bailed her and carried on. But you can go only so fast in a dinghy, and because the Gulf Stream moves north, we just caught Memory Rock, almost twenty miles north of the harbor at West End. Without *Minitaur* and her good diesel engine, we would not have been able to get south at all and Bermuda would have been the next stop. Well, it would have come to a vote. We could have zigged back to northern Florida.

2100. Up anchor and away, cool easterly breeze, heading for open sea.

DAY 46. A gray sky, like a floating oil slick. A sudden huge cloud almost overhead. Waterspout! This is a tornado over water that sucks black strands of ocean up into a dark funnel. Winds can be over two hundred miles per hour in it, and there is nothing to do but watch (and look out for Dorothy?). What a sight! What fear! Carol comes on deck and screams. I tell her there is absolutely nothing we can do. It moves randomly and too fast to avoid. I try to convince her that there is something wonderful about fate and that things will turn out exactly the right way. "Screw that," she says.

Now, night is falling and more dark clouds are looming. Suddenly, this trip seems overwhelming, and the choices I'll have to make too difficult. I find myself full of fears, nightmares of going aground, questions about what course to take, and insecurities because I don't have Dad around to give his approval on every decision I make. The waterspout left us alone, but what's ahead?

DAY 47. Calm night—we drift for twelve hours and sleep under bright stars with the sails on deck like huge leaves.

DAY 48. A satisfying dawn shot of Polaris fixed our latitude at 26° 13' north. We're on a line between Grand Bahama Island and Great Island, above Bimini. The sun sits like a half egg on the horizon. Tropical storm Arthur is raging near Barbados and being watched by me and many others.

To find a lighthouse is such a thrill. This part of the ocean is tricky. *Sparrow* is much bigger than the dinghy, but the problem is the same. *Sparrow* is averaging four knots, and we are heading east, leaving Florida behind and hitting the Bahamas. The Gulf Stream has its maximum velocity here, being bottlenecked between Florida and the Bahamas. It's moving north at an average of three knots— so we move sideways across the treadmill. Add to this a wind from the southeast. We end up doing a sort of crab dance, so to actually get where we want is also a thrill.

DAY 49. Becalmed for twenty-four hours—floating motionless on a very clear sea. Carol wants to go home and is crying. I want the horizon to appear so I can use my sextant. I feel selfish at not knowing what to say to calm her, but I also enjoy seeing someone cosmopolitan— who does all those things I don't like—suffer. That's a cruel streak in me that I usually try not to see, and it comes, I suppose, from mixed feelings about my mother's success at dealing with people, an ability I certainly lack. All my life, she's been the center of every party, a woman who can be two days horizontal with a 102° fever and then spring up miraculously for a six-hour late-night festivity. Whatever my resentment of this, I think I will defer the analysis of it to the couch.

"Carol," I say, trying to calm her, "the hurricane is way over that way. Don't worry."

"Hurricane? *What hurricane?*" (Eyes huge.)

"Um, nothing, don't worry." Carol cries more. Later she calls me the big brother she never wanted to have.

The rubber frog I hid in the toilet just worked. Carol is out of control with terror, me with giggles.

Sailing into Lucaya, Grand Bahama, we can see wrinkles on rocks thirty feet down and I'm all antsy. It looks like I can touch bottom without wetting my elbows and we're sailing over it!

I accidently drop my new Polaroid sunglasses in and stand there going, "Shit . . . Damn . . . Darn . . ." and then Carol says, "What are you looking at, dummy? Jump in!" So I do and get them.

During the night she wakes me. "Dan—um—sorry to wake you, but I think there's a beach ahead." I think to myself, "Jeez, she doesn't know *anything* about sailing." I come on deck, see the beach, and say, "I knew that," and change course.

DAY 51. By noon, Nassau hotels emerge in a fuzzy, mirage-like image on the horizon, pulling trees and hilltops after them. Paradise Island. The wind dies, and we slowly sail in. Under a bridge in the main harbor we spend a half-hour exactly stationary, moving through the water at three knots, against the current of three knots. Passers-by stop and look at Carol in her bikini—I'm grateful for their distraction, being, as usual, concerned with my seamanship image. Finally a little motorboat nuzzles up to our stern and pushes us east of the bridge, where we anchor.

Ashore we have a quick fright as a car nearly runs over us; in the Bahamas they drive on the wrong side of the road. We find a tacky restaurant and have great conch fritters.

DAY 52. I put Carol on a plane. I come back to *Sparrow* and enjoy the solitude, the quiet. Tiger mr'ows up to my ear and says, "So *that* was a girl, huh?" "Yeah," I say. "Amazing, isn't it?"

Lisa, what are you doing in my dreams? Still beautiful,

tempting, and holding back from me. Our relationship lived in that tension, but how I want to be committed to something like that. I remember how vulnerable I became, sensitive to a sideways glance from you. And it's no surprise I've stayed away from people since then, scared little boy of eighteen, retreating behind acts that protect me while, in truth, it's like wrapping cheese in plastic and putting it in the sun—it smolders and rots and takes a long time to stink. (Just don't open the bag.) So I become cold and funny and very alone. Like cheese in a bag.

DAY 60. Hawksbill Cay. On a lonely spit of beach, where bottles wash up, a little yellow warbler pretends her wing is broken, leading me away from her nest.

I anchored here last night at dark—angry because I wanted to get in to Warderick Cay where, the guidebook says, under a full moon (tonight), the cay is haunted by a church congregation singing hymns. But no. It was banana pancakes and fruit flies for supper.

Now I'm standing on this tiny beach holding a five-foot-long spear on which is pierced a wiggling, gasping, silver-and-blue creature. He's dying a horrible death. One moment he was swimming around me, the most curious thing he'd seen on his reef all day, and then in the next, a dull thud tore a hole in him the size of a piece of fire coral (a nickel in my world). I swim onto the beach quickly because I am scared of sharks. I put the fish in my mesh bag and feel awful. It's easier to open a can of tuna, but there's death in that, too. Standing here on the beach, I suddenly realize I don't have my big scuba knife, and I feel helpless.

I love being self-sufficient. To me that has always meant having the right *stuff* for any emergency. My car back home contains, along with 60 percent of my clothing, a canteen, jumper cables, six gallons of extra gas, windshield-wiper fluid, a shovel, two knives (one hidden), pliers, odd tools, an electric razor, a can opener, soda, sev-

eral cans of food, binoculars, a quart of rum, a quart of
paint, a sleeping bag, two combs, a tape deck, a searchlight, an emergency medical "Crash Kit," two flashlights,
nail cutters, vitamins, a key to the windows of the Connecticut College library, twenty other keys to assorted bicy-
cles, boats, and houses (including one to the observatory at
the same college and its big telescope), two hundred feet of
parachute cord, thirty feet of quarter-inch nylon, winter
boots, three sets of foul-weather gear, toothbrush, toothpaste, old herpes medicine (you never know), matches,
money, a sewing kit, two knapsacks, small hedge trimmers,
a condom (again, you never know), toothpicks, Q-tips,
toilet paper, aspirin, half a Valium, a Bible, several other
books ranging from *Winnie the Pooh* to *Beyond Good and
Evil*, a Baudelaire quotation, three cardboard boxes, six
hundred feet of sail twine, a camera, a flute, two pairs of
sneakers, one set of dress shoes, shoelaces, film, and an
assortment of screws—I mean, you could drop me in the
middle of Africa with my car and I'd either drive out or set
up an entire new Western civilization based on consump-
tion. So when I notice that my knife is not strapped Tarzan-
like to my thigh, I picture my two boyhood heroes, James
Bond and G.I. Joe, scorning me.

When the Bogeyman I've been arming myself against all
my life does show up, it'll be in the one moment I'm naked
and vulnerable, as in my old Freudian dreams where my
gun shoots only rubber bullets and the nozzle wilts. When
I go camping, for example, I am armed to the teeth. I love
to be close to nature and run through the woods wearing
nothing except for a seven-inch survival knife lashed to my
thigh. Three more years on the couch?

And then there's my watch. It's waterproof to six hundred feet. It has five alarms, a polarized face, and is made
of plastic so it can't rust. I don't have to change the battery until I'm thirty-one years old. I once read that para-
noid people are so lonely that they invent their fear to

imagine someone cares enough about them to want to hurt them.

More than five hundred miles to Jamaica. Island hopping in paradise. But I want to get there, get Dad on board, and go for the Pacific.

DAVID

My memories of Panama are perspiration, mosquitoes that could kill you without the yellow fever, and more awful Chinese food. We were still building while we waited—a vegetable bin forward, better cockpit drains, a few more hand grips near the hatch. Dan carefully flaked our 160 feet of 5/16" anchor chain into a shallow bilge compartment under the mast, where the weight of the chain would be lower in the boat and farther aft, nearer the center of the hull.

Sparrow's interior was by now a fine success, well thought out, and not conventional. Everyone talks of light and airy interiors. Airy, yes. But light, for a sea boat? Not all of it. Let's have a bit of cozy and snug, a bit dark for day-sleepers. As a matter of even more importance, we wanted a locker where wet gear could be hung before entering the main living area—and never have to drag wet suits through to a locker at the forward end. And a boot locker—clothing tends to drift around in a small space and boots are the worst offenders, the meatballs in the spaghetti of wet everything.

When we began back in New London, *Sparrow*'s long doghouse had two full-sized windows on each side. We covered these with teak panels, and cut two portholes on each side, aft. Light would be concentrated aft in the galley area. Then we raised the galley floor two and one-half inches, making a tiny but vital step-down into the forward "salon" of the berths (seats), table, and books. What a precious step that is—no wet gear goes forward of that room-divide. In our minds it's as much a barrier as a full bulk-head.

To starboard as you come down into the galley area there was a six-and-a-half-foot-long quarter berth at sitting level. But who would sit there, at sea, under the hatch and opposite the stove? And all that wasted space above it! We raised the berth eighteen inches, creating a huge two-level chart bin underneath, plus ample space for tools. Then we shortened the quarter berth to six feet and moved it aft six inches, creating room for a twelve-inch bin—small but enough for foul-weather gear. We made reach-in lockers above and behind the bin for the dozens of items one needs near the cockpit. It has worked wonderfully. Without an engine in the way, and without a space-wasting stair, there is a real galley with the stove to port, and the quarter berth and lockers to starboard. The high berth rim is a brace to help keep you on your feet when *Sparrow* is bouncing. At sea the berth would be jammed with gear, but at home it would be fine for sleeping. The struggle to put on and take off our oilies takes place in this little area, and not in the living space. To do otherwise would be like having a ski chalet without a vestibule so that, laden with gear and wet snow, you would charge directly into the living room. In fact, if *Sparrow* were four feet longer, my preference would not be for greater accomodation, but for a larger "wet-room"—a teak-lined locker room aft, bare, but with benches and hooks where one could more comfortably wriggle out of wet clothing. To me it's strange that designers of larger boats don't make this a priority.

Deeper in the boat, in the salon, it is cozy. A bit of air hatch is overhead, through which we can view the mast, and two tiny ports on the front of the doghouse command the foredeck. There is a port in the aft hatch, too, so from below all of *Sparrow*'s deck rig is visible. We covered the bulkheads, walls, and ceilings with thin planking, insulating where we could. No fiberglass shows in the warm cabin; I've seen glass cabins so ugly that I'd prefer to stay on deck in a hurricane. We bent an arch of ash, laminated with a few strips of mahogany to make it handsome, and this braces the deck-stepped mast. We laminated half-arches, which would reinforce the doghouse should *Sparrow* fall hard, as had *Vertue XXXV*.

We felt good about our craft. The small heat stove worked. The Navik self-steerer was excellent when used properly. Six lines went to the top of the mast. Four of the six could handle jibs; four of the six could work for the main halyard or topping lift. Our navigation lights—red, green, and white—were on the masthead, plus a tiny white light to glow on the wind pennant. We did not install spreader lights (to illuminate the deck), and I just read an account where a good sailor turns them on in gales. Why? To ruin his night vision if someone goes over? Perhaps dockside parties, or an on-deck emergency appendectomy. There's always a trace of light at sea, but if you don't know your boat entirely by feel, you shouldn't go out at night.

We had three anchors and three compasses. We made seat cushions from one cow's hide that we bought in a tannery in Mexico. All the drawers had sturdy turnbuttons to keep them in. We had long handrails below that we could grab without aiming. In the narrow cabin we could hold both rails at once; in *Sparrow* we never had far to fall, and that's not merely funny—it would count in dirty weather, when *Sparrow* would be jumping and corkscrewing in waves that sometimes seemed to have ninety-degree angles. We had put in a twelve-inch-deep sink and an icebox for future, gentler cruising when guests might hope for fresh milk or a cold soda, luxuries we never needed at sea. Dan's electrical system resembled his model railroad, and under the cockpit he built racks for two big storage batteries, with straps to keep them in if we rolled too far. There was a five-gallon tank for kerosene, with a pump and enough thin hose to reach the stove. It was a good job; we were proud of *Sparrow*.

Thomas, a slight and attractive young Panamanian, adopted us and ran errands and located services for our remaining chores. He had been caught sneaking into Texas and had spent a year in a Mexican prison. "We ate leftover food from the finest hotel in Mexico City," he said. "All gourmet food, but it came to us in garbage cans, and the fillets would be mixed in with the coffee grounds and the discarded drinks. A big gourmet soup."

The boat was ready, and now we turned to the business of crossing to the Pacific Ocean. Dan managed the endless paperwork that would clear our tiny vessel through the canal. He had never been able to work his way through application forms before, but now he dealt with twelve different inspectors and filled out sixteen forms. *Sparrow* was to be precisely described. Our measurer was a young woman. There was much leering by her fellow officers when she was introduced to us, before she crawled with her tape measure into *Sparrow*'s tiny spaces, and even more after we walked back with her to the customs office.

There are many regulations to follow, and we were told in no uncertain terms that boats cannot carry sail through the canal. An engineless craft can hire a tugboat for over one thousand dollars, but Thomas located a fisherman who would rent us his outboard motor, and come along with his son-in-law to help us through. We built a sturdy bracket for the engine. Six people were needed to bring the tiny boat through the canal: the steersman (me), the pilot supplied by canal authorities, and three to handle lines— Dan, the fisherman's son-in-law, and one we would have to find. Our sixth would be the fisherman, to lovingly supervise his new 25 hp Suzuki.

Our last two days were busy with dozens of trips to the canal's offices and completing the final paperwork; then we floated *Sparrow* onto an ancient marine railway, hauled her out and cleaned her bottom, our last chance. Mostly we cleaned off the thick muck of harbor oil, which is always present in Cristobal, but especially thick for us due to an unusually generous spill just as we arrived—an Exxon representative handed out bottles of special oil cleaner that worked miraculously well, and that made us feel like we were part of a wholesome television commercial. Our sixth man, Carlos, joined us in time to help haul *Sparrow* out. His story was that he was a Nicaraguan pilot who had been shot down. "Once too often," remarked Dan, when Carlos dove into the putrid water to carry lines between docks as we secured *Sparrow* in the hauling cradle.

On our last night in Cristobal we bought dinner for two young sailing couples at the awful Chinese-Mex restaurant. One pair was off to Australia to watch the America's Cup races. Their future didn't seem to be fully linked to the sea. We wondered if the other couple would ever come ashore—he talked incessantly of his skills as a sailor, diver, and boat builder, and told Dan how to defeat sharks. He walked two steps ahead of the lady, and she never spoke when she was with him. He mentioned her only once, when he said that she cried when they lost a boat (a huge surging wave uprooted their anchor and smashed the boat on a beach). He knew of a stack of wonderful mahogany and dreamed of building another boat and selling this one, which we guessed was hers, and we guessed that the money was hers.

It seemed we would never get started. Dan, nearing the end of his job list: "I've done three jobs already today and that's counting only one job twice." Then, we went to make final arrangements for the outboard. The fisherman lived in a little community pinched between a railroad siding and the harbor shore. You saw it suddenly as you walked around the corner of a warehouse. The homes were giant wooden packing crates, joined together and roofed.

White sheets and white clothing on clotheslines moved gently in the wind, the sun glowing through the cloth, a startling Fellini-like image. For the first moment in Panama I had a sense of seeing lives and homes rather than suppliers or warehouses.

Transit day arrived, finally, and our crew assembled. The outboard engine was bolted on and Mr. Santa-Marie, a thin, delicate-looking young man who was to be our pilot, came on board. He looked and spoke so much like a Panamanian stage director I once worked with that I became nervous about the practical aspects of the job ahead. At ten the pilot's walkie-talkie spoke out and we cast off. Thomas waved goodbye, with "take me with you" in his eyes. It is a statement that I have seen in eyes around the world.

Little boats don't lock through the Panama Canal alone, as it would be a waste of water—each lock holds enough water to float the *Queen Elizabeth II*. Our big sister ship was the *Unimar* from Callao, Peru. We turned into the main channel and she was there, a perfect rendezvous. At the first gate, where a lock-hand offered to sell drugs to Dan, the pilot reminded us to be careful about handling the lines; the surge of water into the gigantic locks can toss and smash a small craft. Two days earlier a line-handler's thumb had been whipped off. We made fast to an eighty-foot tug that was in the first lock with us and the *Unimar*. Mr. Santa-Marie suggested to the captain that he move us to the next lock, instead of casting off as he moved ahead. He refused. "A bullshit captain," Santa-Marie confided.

A six-foot tarpon jumped astern. Pelicans hunted in the turmoil of the lock's water, the thuds as they hit mixing with the gulls' screams as they dove to a surface whipped by small fish. The giant steel boxes were like coffins, the unnatural upward heave of water, in the immense fixed rectangles, was as disorienting as an earthquake, and *Sparrow*, for the first time, seemed small—a chip.

Once we were clear of the first group of locks, the pilot

took us through shortcuts in Gatun Lake and we reconnected with the faster *Unimar*. We ate the sandwiches Dan and I had been instructed to supply. Mist and then blinding rain closed off the sights to us, and we sped from buoy to buoy, hardly seeing the canal. Night was falling. "*Mañana?*" said Santa-Marie to our fisherman as we entered Gaillard Cut, and the engine whined a note higher, and *Sparrow*'s bow lifted—hull speed, six and one-half knots. Dan and I had read a good book on the canal, David G. McCullough's *The Path Between the Seas*, but now we barely saw it.

Night fell at the step-down in the Miraflores Locks. Mr. Santa-Marie had advanced us, and we were ahead of the *Unimar*, descending with a giant tanker. There were only a few feet to spare under the looming bow, the scene crazily etched by orange lights, broken and scattered in the drizzle like glowing thistles. Then, for the first time, *Sparrow* was floating on the waters of the Pacific.

In darkness we docked at the yacht club in Balboa. The fisherman's son-in-law hoisted the engine to his shoulder, and the crew and pilot walked up the gangplank to catch the last train back to Colón. We were towed to a mooring by the club's workboat, and bobbed miserably all night in the wash of big ships coming out into the Pacific, revving up to their full speed. Between ship passings we slewed in the strong currents of the sixteen-foot Balboa tide.

On October 24, which we hoped would be our last night ashore, we shopped in Balboa and Panama City. Parts of General Noriega's city were modern, neat, military. We found a McDonald's—which we enjoyed, guessing it was probably our last fast-food fix. Dan had mail at the yacht club and a package from his sister. This young man, who considers himself such an outsider, doted on his mail. For his first year after high school, before he entered Connecticut College, he studied at the new state university in Olympia, Washington, three thousand miles from home. I feared he had no stimulating companions, and I wrote a letter to him every day. I needed it. He didn't, and he didn't remember. "Mail, sure—but every day, Dad?"

The next day there was a lively squall in the harbor and waves crashed onto the club porch. We would have been unable to work our way out of the harbor. It was maddening—the Pacific was there, and we were land-held. The next morning, October 26, grayed to mist and light rain.

"C'mon, Dan," I said. "A British boat only sails in rain!" We cast off the big mooring buoy and moved downcurrent into the Gulf of Panama.

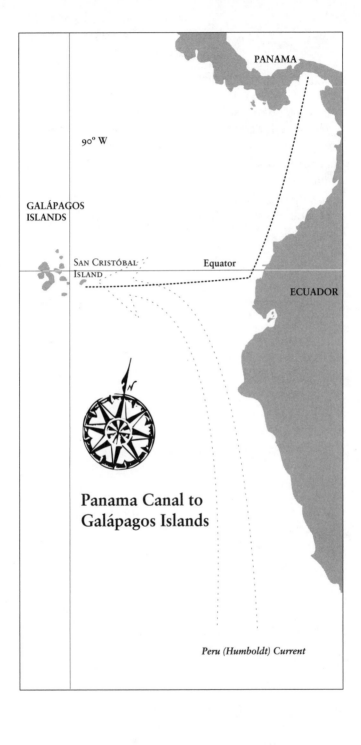

PANAMA

90° W

GALÁPAGOS
ISLANDS

San Cristóbal
Island

Equator

ECUADOR

Panama Canal to
Galápagos Islands

Peru (Humboldt) Current

5 IN THE PACIFIC

By day, fear; by night, terror.
  —British small-boat lore

DAVID

The Humboldt Current, now called the Peru Current or the South Equatorial Current, sweeps up the west coast of South America and turns left, out into the Pacific, at the equator just south of Guayaquil. It can be three hundred miles wide, and it's cold. It strokes the Galápagos with coolness the way the Gulf Stream warms the British Isles, which explains some of the diversity of life on those equatorial islands. North of the Humboldt, in the notch where Central America joins South America, another movement of water, the Equatorial Counter Current, moves to the east toward the continent. Our strategy, typical of these small-boat voyages, was to work down the coast of Colombia. Close to shore there was little current. Then we would ride the Humboldt out to the Galápagos. This can be a tedious and lengthy passage, only eleven hundred miles direct, but the area can be windless.

It rained lightly, and it rained heavily, but the wind was steady, against us. Short but steep seas held us back, although little *Sparrow* bucked through them with surprising power. We zigged toward shore during the days and zagged out at night. The lurching progress unsettled me for the first three days, but Dan had his sea legs. We planned to follow the advice we'd heard in Panama and work down the coast to about three degrees south of the equator, about one hundred and eighty miles, and then stand out for the Islands.

We saw shore lights behind us at night, punctuated by shore-hugging cargo ships. Ahead of us during the days we could see only a mist-shrouded, blue-gray land shape. An edge of the sun would appear exactly on cue for Dan's sextant shots, but otherwise we plowed through a mixed soup, not gourmet, of dark gray water, steel clouds, gray mist, drizzle, and spray. We put back an average of eighty-five miles a day, which is good for uphill work, but we hadn't really started. Joseph Conrad explains this in *The Mirror of the Sea*:

> The Departure is distinctly a ceremony of navigation. A ship may have left her port some time before; she may have been at sea, in the fullest sense of the phrase, for days; but for all that, as long as the coast she was about to leave remained in sight, a southern-going ship of yesterday had not in the sailor's sense begun the enterprise of a passage . . . Departure, if not the last sight of the land, is, perhaps, the last professional recognition of the land on the part of the sailor . . . It is not the ship that takes her Departure; the seaman takes his Departure by means of cross-bearings which fix the place of the first tiny pencil-cross on the white expanse of the track-chart, where the ship's position at noon shall be marked by just such another tiny pencil-cross for every day of her passage . . .

Conrad goes on to speak of the depression at the start of the voyages, of many captains who dove into their cabins for three, four, and five days and then emerged with serene brows. It was not, for us, the departure from loved ones, it was simply the time needed to fall into routine, over-coming early voyage queasiness and sleeplessness. Three days out and about two hundred and forty miles down the coast, I began to feel well enough to start tasks other than ship handling. There was a bit of sun, and I sewed straps to hold down *Sparrow*'s bunk cushions if she rolled over.

On the sixth night out from Panama, zagging away from shore, the air felt cool with a sense of distance in the cool, not just rain dampness. The wind shifted slightly and for the first time we were not pinching as close to the wind as *Sparrow* can sail. On change of watch I asked Dan if we could step out for the Islands. We were sixty miles south of the equator, one hundred and twenty miles north of our planned turning point. But even vast currents, and the winds that move with them, shift their paths. It felt right. "Let's go," he said, and we eased sheets and headed west. She started to move as if she'd exhaled and started down a hill. The distant lights of the continent faded in an hour. We took Departure. Our Pacific voyage had begun.

DAN

DAY 107. Sailing upwind down the Colombia coast, and it's lively work. It's impossible to do anything but wedge to leeward and hang on; every sixth or so wave, the deck is awash in swirling, bubbling green water. Dad hands me a cup of tea which I tell him tastes exactly like a used pipe cleaner. He says, "Well, *I've* never sucked on a pipe cleaner, but now I don't have to." I drink it—the water is precious. Each cup has value.

I like all the food aboard. The bins under each settee-berth are overfull with cans of everything, bought with Carol in Florida and leveled up in Panama. It's like, "OK God, all is together here," and the game is to adapt to the environment—stay alive, keep *Sparrow* moving. I'm wor-ried about Tiger—I have only a week of cat food, so I'm not using it and trying to get him to eat avocado, peanut butter, macaroni and cheese, etc. I think when he gets hungrier he will.

It's been a lonely watch—big waves roll under and swoosh toward shore, and a voice says, "I want to go with you little wave . . ." We are far from other people but close to ourselves out here. I'm concentrating on making heat. My body struggles to stay ahead of the 0300 cold.

Getting around below is like tree climbing—you need to have three points of your body secured at once, and even the cat makes dashes only to places where he can get wedged in. I share my lunch with him—Dad's feeling lousy and not eating. He has the watch now, and he's on deck shouting commands. This seems to cheer him on these gray days when we sail three miles to make less than two in the direction we really want to go. "On the foredeck, look sharp there! Aloft, ready to wear ship—main braces—*haul!*" Then down to me, "You've got to learn how to give orders to this scurvy bunch, Dan." He's been on watch too long; it's my turn.

The high point of today was poking a hole in Dad's can of cola so it dribbled down his chest when he drank it. The low point was he didn't notice. Well, he finally did and we laughed hysterically for a half-hour. I suppose this proves that there isn't much entertainment out here. Dad and I are doing well together now. I still become unreasonable (furious) when he acts helpless—unable to find a pencil he's sitting on or a book he's looking right at. But we're settling in.

I wedge myself in to write—feeling wonderful now because although I'm not "doing" anything, the boat's moving and this is because of me. So I *should* feel wonderful, but—thank you Judeo-Christian work ethic—those voices inside me are sort of mumbling reproachfully. "Screw you," I tell them, and they quiet some. Tiger steps off the cabin top onto my shoulder, nestles into my jacket, and settles right on my chest. He looks up. "Whatcha doing?"

"Writing about this very moment," I say.

"Am I in it?" he says, chewing the edge of my notebook.

"Yah, but if you piss on my sleeping bag again I'll come back and edit you out." He closes his eyes and smiles, knowing he can and I won't.

DAY 110. Took departure today, in the Conradian sense, and then we celebrated Halloween with a double candy ration. The candy is the yellow, orange, and white corn candy that Julia sent to Balboa for our Halloween. We're rationed to three pieces each per day. The party never really took off, but we all came in costume. I was a pirate, wearing a bandana with a knife held between my teeth. Dad drew an arched black cat body on a piece of paper and put Tiger's head through a hole in it. His costume seemed to be that he was holding the cat, but he told me to notice that he was holding a fork upright and that made him Poseidon.

Tiger has grown more affectionate at night. When I'm lying in the cockpit trying not to move so warmth stays in the pockets made by my curling, I say, "Tiger, come here." He gets up, stretches, and tentatively puts his front paws on my throat and does his kneading exercises. Then he walks onto my head and sits on my neck with his head lying so that his whiskers just tickle my nose. He sometimes manages to set a whisker *inside* my nose, which itches worse than anything.

We begin to fall into the routine of daily maintenance and improvements. We lace on the weather cloths that we had prepared in New London. These are rectangles of Dacron cloth thirty inches wide and eight feet long that attach to the lifelines at either side of the cockpit and across its aft end. These will help to keep us dry. The tightly stretched top wire of the lifeline is thirty inches above the deck, and there is a middle strand as well. If it was any lower you'd simply spiral as you were swept off the boat, but any higher and it would interfere too much with working the boat with its narrow side decks.

Dad's polished some of the brass below, which means he thinks he's in the British Navy. We run out three hundred feet of spare line that became kinked when we took it out of its factory coil the wrong way. Towing it eases out the kinks. I label cans of food with a magic marker in case the paper wrappers get soaked off. We've settled into six-hour watches, and I'm on midnight to dawn, or 6:00 A.M., and the less-defined noon-to-six watch. The motion is invisible to us now, and almost without thought, my body constantly shifts, tenses, and relaxes to keep me upright and balanced.

Sailors used to raid the Galápagos Islands and stack the great turtles on their backs like sacks of rice in the hold of the ship. A two- to five-hundred-pound turtle would live up to a year without food or drink—just live till he was eaten. What a miserable year of dull turtle thoughts.

I hear news and wonder how the world is doing without me. Lots of deaths.

I was an emergency medical technician for a few years and one time did cardiopulmonary resuscitation on a huge black woman who could not have been more distant in form, and no doubt experience, from anything in my world—someone with whom I had almost nothing in common. She had been horribly injured in a car accident. Finally the doctors gave up and went off to dinner, leaving a nurse and me to clean up the results of the last violent attempt to save her that had been made by fifteen people brandishing needles, tubes, and machines. After that, I saw her in my mind as she must have once been: a little girl running to her mother with a scratched knee. Every one of that woman's experiences over her forty years of life were as rich to her as each of mine to me. The nurse and I put her false teeth back in. I tied her arms over her chest and her feet together with white bandage. Her legs were broken, snapped at the shin, and the ragged bones stuck through the skin like wood through torn canvas. I prayed desperately that she'd cough and wake up. Even though she would then have had to feel the pain in her legs. But she never moved. The doctors had not been wrong when they pronounced her dead. I could hear her daughter screaming in the next room—she survived the accident.

Near death isn't death, though. It's life. The contrast is always striking. Flattening a bug is easy with your foot—even if you swat a mosquito with your hand—the whole death just rubs off, it's so small. But try *pinching* a cockroach to death. No, we don't do that, we feed it poison. Our loved pets visit the vet to be "put to sleep."

I shot my dog. A little, white, fluffy thing I got when I was ten—my childhood companion who, by the time I finished college, was blind and deaf, who could only eat and shit. It hurt me to keep her shell alive when no one treated her like a living thing—she was a "burden," and there was no room for her in my family's fast life. I could not bring her to a strange place to get an injection to die. Like children, dogs sense things no matter how you pretend. Dad dug the grave, and one day during a normal walk in the little field she loved, I quickly shot her and gently lowered her into it. Actually, that's a lie. It was all a little too intense for me. You see the justification and perhaps the resolve it took—but not the surprise and intense reality of seeing blood spurt from the ears I'd lovingly scratched thousands of times, watching heaving last breaths and quivers. I emptied all the bullets into her, scared she might feel the pain. My vision was blurred by tears, but I knew I was committed after I'd pulled the trigger the first time and there could be no stopping, as if I'd fallen from a cliff and was watching the ground come up to meet me. I threw dirt over her quickly and cried it out for two hours with the moon full. I do not regret what I did. It was my choice, and I chose not to watch a friend decay.

All that is what I mean about death. It's very abstract until you get the smell on you. The smell of that woman—my open palms pumping rhythms on her chest—that odor lasted a week beyond the first day of frequent hand-washings. Each meal I ate was interrupted by her image as I raised my fork and smelled my hand. And now there's no white bundle of dog to feed scraps to under the table, either.

Sparrow is sailing beautifully in strong and steady winds on a line just south of the equator. We feel like the ancients, running down our latitude—once we've found our line and steer due west, the island can't dodge out of our way. Long and blended surges. The Navik steers us perfectly. This is good weather and our daily runs are about 145 miles. On November 5 we reset our clocks. This is for our convenience, and keeps Dad's evening watch at sunset and my dawn watch at sunrise. It has nothing to do with navigation, because we use Greenwich mean time for that. We're not going to be jet-lagged on this trip.

DAVID

Dan used a small computer, the size of a pocket calculator, to work out his celestial sights. It stored much of the almanac information, which sped up the process that normally involves looking up figures in books of logarithm tables and adding and subtracting various corrections. The computer keeps the big books on their shelves and off the tiny cabin table. The tough part is always the sight itself, steadying the view of the sun or moon or star in the eyepiece and distinguishing between the distant horizon and the crest of a nearby wave. Almost half the time, in a boat of this size, you are below these crests. I undertook to understand the computer instructions because Dan would have put this off. And I labored to understand them well, because once he grasped the very first step, I knew he would say, "OK, Dad, *enough, enough!*"

Celestial navigation is not an intellectual height to scale. Taking the sight itself, on a small jumping boat, is the art. To work it out, one must understand a few of the simplest astronomical terms, and possess only the ability to add and subtract. Some good sailors have written that they know of no simple text that combines theory and practice, but they must have missed Mary Blewitt's *Celestial Navigation for Yachtsmen.* An English solicitor and amateur sailor, she has written the best text I've ever read on any subject, and the easy-to-follow examples in her thin and inexpensive volume cover every situation I can imagine for a small boat.

Here is some theory, in a few oversimplified paragraphs for those of you who wonder what that mariner is doing, squinting into that curious device.

Imagine the sun (moon, star) circling around the earth. Forgive me, Copernicus, that's the way we do it. The sun is a round grape, the earth is an orange. Connect the center of the grape and the center of the orange with a taut thread. The point where this line, the thread, pierces the surface of the orange is called the GP, or geographical position. This GP moves constantly as the sun or other body goes around the earth. There is only one GP at any second, and this exact point, for every second of every day, is found from tables in an almanac you buy for each year.

You observe the sun in the sextant, measuring its height above the horizon with a movable mirror—after cranking the mirror image of the sun down to touch the horizon, you check the marking on the sextant to measure the angle you've cranked. You mark the exact second when you're satisfied that the globe is just kissing the horizon. You know, from the almanac, the point on the earth that the sun is directly over—the GP—at that second. So, you now have two angles, the one you caught in your sight, and a right angle (ninety degrees), because at the GP, the point directly under the sun, the sun is obviously straight up. And you know a distance—from the surface of the earth to the earth's center. As you remember from geometry, a triangle can be solved with two sides and an angle, or two angles and a side (distance), and here you have that. The side of the triangle you now want to find is the side lying on the surface of the earth between where you took your sight and the GP. That side is your distance from the GP, and from what you know, simple tables tell it to you. Take a moment to look at this diagram; it will bring you back to basic high-school geometry.

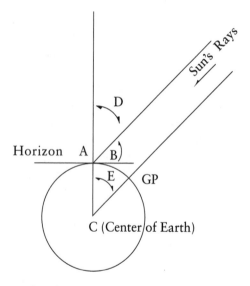

You are on your ship at A.
Angle of sun by sextant is B.
Center of the Earth is C.
GP is the third angle of the triangle ACGP.
Angle D is 90° minus angle B.
Angles D and E are the same.

You know position GP from the almanac, and you know the lengths C to A and C to GP. Knowing two sides and an angle of a triangle, you can solve for the third side, the distance A to GP.

This is the basic idea, though in the development of the theory it becomes slightly complex. For example, your GP may be thousands of miles away—too far to draw accurately on a chart. So you use basic geometry again and advance it toward you based on your time zone, establishing a nearby surrogate GP. Also, there is azimuth—the direction of the sun from you in compass degrees. Again, tables and simple addition or subtraction make that easy. Of course, the surface of the earth is part of a sphere, not a circle, so spherical and not ordinary high-school geometry is used—but again the tables do that, not you. So, observing angle and time, you turn to such and such a page, add or subtract, then do it once more. Or, let the tiny computer do this for you, leading you with step-by-step questions. You take into account some simple corrections—the height of your eye above the water, and so forth. Finally you can draw a line on the chart. You're somewhere on that line. But it's a long line, many miles long. To pinpoint your position, you need another sight to establish another line that will intersect the first one. The moon might be up when you shoot the sun, so you have an instant cross. Or you can wait a couple of hours and let the sun move. Shoot again— the new line will cross the old one, which you draw again, adding to it the distance and the direction you've covered since the first sight (you know this from your compass direction and your estimated speed).

You can also shoot certain stars and planets, chosen by the almanac-makers because of their brightness and good heights at the time you need them. A dandy pinwheel of lines, all crossing at one point, is a thrilling small achievement. But you can only shoot stars when the horizon is sharp and the stars visible. Perhaps ten minutes each dusk or dawn in good weather.

Two kinds of shots are easy: a "noon sight" and a shot of the North Star, Polaris. If you are in the North Atlantic in winter, for example, the sun is due south at noon, and the almanac tells you exactly how far south of the equator it is. You don't need to know the exact time. These noon sights get tough when you are directly under the sun—if you are on the equator when the sun rides along it about September 21, for example. But it can be done. ("Dan can do it" is my interpretation of that phrase now.) Shooting Polaris is easy too, because it stays close to one place, with a minor correction that is easily added or subtracted; again, you can get latitude without exact time. But you have to be in the Northern Hemisphere to do this, and when that star sank below the horizon for the southern-going old-timers, a friend was lost. (Of course they knew why. That "earth is flat" nonsense was already discarded in Columbus's time—they just weren't sure how *big* the globe was.) We took a dandy Polaris shot at dawn when we were sailing that nine-foot dinghy from Miami to the Bahamas. The course lies in a northeasterly direction, but the current sweeps north at about three knots, and a dinghy won't sail at much more than three knots. So we were sailing east and being dragged north. The star sight let us know how far north we'd been swept, but until the sun came up and gave us a sense of how far east we'd gone, we didn't know if we were holding course or if we were being swept up past the Bahamas.

Most ocean yachts now carry systems that show you where you are by pushing a button, and this handy connection to a satellite reads out your longitude and latitude, give or take a few yards.

When Dan and I sailed the dinghy across the Gulf Stream, we had a marvelous night target, two great planets extraordinarily bright and close together, twins that would have been a once-in-a-century omen to the old sky-watchers. We were not set up to do planets or stars other than Polaris in the little craft or in her mother ship, our twenty-two-foot catboat, which did have a radio direction-finder to help us in these well-signaled waters. On the way back from the Bahamas, I asked the navigator of our airliner what the planets were. You could see them at that moment from the starboard ports. "We don't learn celestial anymore," he said sheepishly, "we just push buttons and our position shows on a screen." He soon had them from home base by radio: Mars and Jupiter.

Sailing is so many sports: the word is as broad as "walking," if you include scaling K2 as part of walking. Tastes vary in navigation. My friend Jack Evans, a World War II navy veteran, recently piloted his yacht through a murderously complex channel in thick fog, delighting in his skillful and accurate use of his radar. I respect his enjoyment of the sport. And all the more power to those who want a control panel worthy of a 747 set above the navigation table on their boat. It's a perfectly good version of fun, and it spreads the money around. But in Panama we met a sailor who had waited nine weeks for a replacement part for his satellite navigation system. We'd have been on the way to Horn Island by then. It's hard to push off without a fully working ship, which we understood. You lose the enjoyment of perfection, or even competence, when you look at a dead lump of metal, even if you rarely use it. Dan once waited two weeks for an engine part for our catboat. Now we have few such devices. We're always ready to go, a simple ship.

I remember sailing in Maine, in fog, listening for wave sounds or echoes off the rocks, for the bells or whistles on the buoys. My estimated position was confirmed by a subtle sense of wind change as it deflected from an unseen headland. Scary, yes, but our sport is to tune our senses, not our instruments. On that sail, a pretty thirty-six-foot sloop came out of the fog, just yards away, sailing parallel to us. "Are you looking for the yellow mark?" I called over. "We're on SatNav, we don't do buoys," was the answer.

Now we're going to retire our Walker log. This is a small odometer, mounted on our stern rail, that trails a thin braided line that transmits spin from a rotor at its end. So many spins per mile. But Dan's lost two rotors: one snagged on coral, a fish took the other—and they clog with weed and give a faulty reading. We'll judge speed by feel, by watching our wake. Testing against our noon positions, our error is five percent, the same as the log when it's working well. So, even more simply, we sail.

Dan and I never had a shortage of conversation during these long passages. Once we stood on our island at home and argued for ten minutes about whether it was raining. Approaching the Galápagos Islands, we started to bet. Dan was ahead at first. We bet a million dollars that the rain would stop at a certain time and another million on a word that we then looked up in the dictionary. I lost one and won one, but on our tenth day at sea toward the Galápagos, I sold Dan my daily ration of candy corn, three pieces, for a million. Then he claimed I cheated because he saw me eating a piece, but I claimed it was left over from yesterday and, anyway, if he pretended to be asleep and spied on me, it didn't count. The cat was sleeping on his face but somehow he saw out from under the fur. We made a new bet that there would be pizza on the Galápagos. I had a vision of the shipwrecked of all ages staggering ashore after weeks in lifeboats or clinging to logs, croaking, "Junk food! Junk food!"

Twelve days out, as I was just starting watch and Dan was below for his morning nap, he called out, "Dolphins!" He heard them through the sounding drum of *Sparrow*'s fiberglass skin—squeakings, but articulated, and varied and rich. Almost always he heard them before we saw them: bottlenose dolphins, a big school, jumping in pairs, trios, quartets, quintets, sextets, septets, and once a beautiful octet arcing like a rainbow. It was a family group with babies, and they put on a dazzling, colored-crystal show off our port bow. I looked ahead, and there was a blue mountain, in mist, and it was San Cristóbal, Galápagos, our target. Dan made his landfall within an hour of expected time—less mist would have brought it up on the dot—and he was on the correct side of the island. We'd make the turning point into harbor without changing course one degree.

Excitement! Tiger sat up and stared over the bow. Dan took a deck bath, and even I joined him. His enthusiasm to become totally clean was disquieting. To me the process brings to mind words like "adequately" or "reasonably." The water was freezing. How can anyone do this—or worse, swim? I spend thousands of dollars a year from my moderate salary on boats; a boat by definition is something that keeps you from having to swim. I feel failure when I swim.

We stared at the stark, brown-and-tan volcanic island as we sailed smoothly by its south coast. Before sunset, taking bearings on bizarre lava forms that rise straight out of the water, we rounded in and tacked up Wreck Bay. Dan conned us from the bow, determining water depth, Bahama style, from its color and its feel to the eye. We shaved past a sixty-foot French yacht at anchor. "Good evening," I said to a martini-in-hand, heavy gold wristwatch, white pants, blazer, and ascot tie—a generic yachtsman reclining on a deck chair. The smell of olive oil came to us on the dying evening breeze. Damn! If I'd said, "*Bonsoir*," we might have been invited on board for a stylish meal. In the harbor were three yachts, a half-dozen fishing boats, a small rusty Ecuadoran gunboat, and the island supply boat being quietly unloaded. The waterfront was a crescent of two-story buildings, others rising on the embracing hillside—stucco and shutters, a mediocre opera set. But the sound was of children laughing and playing, the purest music. There were swing sets there too, and in the mad Latin style, the youngsters were pendulums swinging above the horizontal —silhouetted against the colored evening sky.

It made me remember a gray street in Calcutta after one performance by the National Theatre of the Deaf, when Chuck Baird, one of our fine actors and a big man, picked up four of the beggar children who had followed him, tugging like weak birds at his elbows—tiny scraps of children, just bits of bone and skin. With one on each shoulder and one hanging from each arm, he danced down the street, and the children laughed and shrieked with joy.

We anchored, were visited briefly and pleasantly by two customs officers, then toasted each other with a finger each of Tia Maria, and turned in to sleep.

The Galápagos Islands

Equator

SANTA CRUZ ISLAND

SAN CRISTÓBAL
ISLAND

SANTA MARIA
ISLAND

90° W

6   THE GALÁPAGOS

*I honestly confess that many times, when I
saw my sails in ribbons and my poor boat
struggling desperately on a raging sea, plunging down terrific precipices, disappearing
under monstrous waves that threaten to swallow her, then pointing her bows to the black
skies as if to implore the mercy of Him whose
will disposes life and death, yes, many times I
said to myself: "If I get away with it this time,
I'll never set foot on a boat again."*

—Marcel Bardiaux, The Four Winds
   of Adventure

DAN

DAY 117

Dear Mom,

Did I ever ask you to forgive me for being such a
jerk/shithead for so many years? I would like to be
forgiven. I want you to know that I forgive you for all
the things that I thought/think you did to me. I do.
You are hereby forgiven and OK as you are. I still have
trouble there—I always want people to be how I
think they should be to be happier . . . You're OK with
me and I love you very much. Love, Dan

According to law, a visiting yacht has only seventy-two
hours to pollute the Galápagos. On the third day we go
ashore and find the port captain.

"Hi," Dad says, "we're sinking. Can we have a couple
more days for repairs?"

"You know," says the port captain, "it amazes me how all you American yachts make it here over rough seas only to sink in our harbors. There are four other sinking yachts here, did you know that?"

"Really? Um . . . wow!"

He gives us an extension, we give him a T-shirt. The guys on the other four yachts told us he likes T-shirts.

This town is pre-touristy still, and not spectacular, except for beautiful children and handsome Indians. The cats look tattered—one that I saw was missing an eye and had claw marks all over its face. In countries like this, there is no prepared cat food, and it was dumb to bet that we'd find some here. Another million lost. But they sell something called *atun*, which is *tuna* spelled sideways. It's cheap.

We row our inflatable dinghy past two seals sunning on the stern deck of a small fishing boat. We do some shopping on the one main street and put our supplies under the dinghy on the beach, and when we come back to row out the food is mushed and half eaten by dogs and the dinghy somehow deflated. Dad asks how we get out to the boat without the pump to blow up the dinghy. We sit and blow it up slowly by mouth. He's smart at hard things but sometimes dumb on easy things. Maybe all dads are like that.

He told me the story once that his father—his dad—bought him a baseball mitt, and it was just a kiddy mitt, and how really hurt he was that his father could do a dopey thing. It took him weeks before he could tell his father, who didn't realize how upset he was. I know that Dad understands all of this, but I give him hell sometimes, and then I feel hurt. We're balancing on a tightrope. On one side is our love as father and son, on the other is the way we work as a grown-up team. And the tightrope, woven from a web of all the things that have happened, holds us up. Partly it's the past and partly it's love, and partly it's keeping *Sparrow* going fast and safely; now that has to be the most unbreakable strand.

There's a particular memory I have, caught between being a photograph and a dim feeling. The photo is lying in a dusty pile of similar images from my early childhood somewhere in one of the remotest attics of my brain, but the feeling it produces stays and is special. I see myself at my grandfather's house near a waterfall. I am wearing a pair of his boxer shorts that I pull up to my armpits. My dad is there also and the three of us are standing on a stone dock with the water rushing coolly by. I wonder which is my dad and which is my grandpa because they look very much alike. It is summer and the trees are green and full of bird sounds, and there is nothing else but the cool water and a feeling that life is perfect. What stands out in my mind is the impression that I was not thinking at all; I was just happy.

This memory is special because it is all I have of my dad's dad, yet I imagine I know him deeply because I can see that he was as close to—perhaps better to say—he *was* my father the same way *I* am my father. That is, we are all together in each of us. He died a few weeks later, but he left me that memory, and I am grateful.

Dad and I are becoming a good boat-handling team. The row to the beach is long, so we use the big stone dock where the freighter unloads supplies. The steps that go right down into the water are slippery. There's always a surge in the harbor and we row the rubber boat near the steps and then suddenly row in to them at the top of the surge. One of us jumps out onto the steps just as the boat is at its highest and, with luck, doesn't get wet. That person has the painter—the bow line of the boat—and he yanks the boat in on the next big wave so the other one can jump out. Then we lift the light boat onto the dock, stowing the oars underneath. Getting in is sort of the reverse. Yesterday I tossed the boat in and lost my grip on the painter. There was the boat drifting away, and before Dad could say, "Asshole!" I made this great jump into it, yelling, "Oars!"

Dad threw them to me like javelins, and the boat was whole again. We admire our teamwork and skill, forgetting, as always, the stupid way we got into the situation in the first place. If you do lots of dumb things, you get to be a hero.

The little town starts with a naval station on the point of the harbor and then one long street curves around the shore of the harbor. There are a few shops. We buy a thermos, but when we open it, it's half full of coffee and we return it. Another street goes up the hill to a church and a small museum with a few badly stuffed birds and lizards. The radiophone station is there, and we call home on a device that may have been first used to bring Frankenstein to life. There is a pool parlor, and two restaurants. Waves break on the bar stretching out from the naval station.

We spend an afternoon with a young man from our Peace Corps. His ambition is to rebuild the musty Natural History Museum, and he's full of the new museum concepts. We learn that "Aha Lava" gets its name from what you say as you walk on it barefoot.

On our last morning on San Cristóbal, we walk uphill, past the radio station, and buy vegetables at the weekly market sale—a shed with a tin roof and concrete stalls. Then we fill our water tanks in a few dinghy trips, using plastic bottles, and we sail.

Our next port, on the island of Santa Cruz, is more built up, a little touristy. We anchor next to *Evora*, a cutter we met in Panama. She's bigger and faster but took fourteen days to make the trip (we took twelve) because she went all the way down to latitude 3° south instead of tacking out with the lift that we sensed.

DAVID

The sail between the islands from Wreck Bay to Porta Ayora was bright and easy, only eight hours. We saw a bosun bird, also called the red-billed tropic bird; I've known them as bosun birds because they carry a marline-spike in their tail, as the salts say—a long tapering feather or two that trail behind. The bird was beautiful and white, and it had the trick of its breed of hovering in the air just above your boat, so still, and suddenly, with great charm, cocking its head and looking down at you.

The harbor at Porta Ayora was better protected. The town had a few more streets—unpaved—and houses and shops that were more deliberately built—more stylishly Spanish, with a touch of ironwork and tiles. There were many more restaurants and shops. And more people. This was the center of the island group and stopping there, we understood why sailors and trippers usually bypass San Cristóbal.

We were visited by the man from the cutter. Dan and I built a spare part for his self-steering gear, which is the same as ours. We had a spare, and I felt selfish; but if we had given him that, he'd have the spare, and we'd have none, so it seemed fair that we built a good facsimile for him. Dan and I have different ideas of spare parts. I like to assemble the means to build a replacement if needed. Dan wants two of everything *plus* the raw materials. That's why our boat was jammed with stuff. It was cleverly stowed and out of the way, but in the tiny curved cupboards it was all stored by size, and the spare toothbrushes ("Sure, Dad, you would have brought extra bristles and wood for the handle and a knife to whittle it and little drill bits to make the tiny holes to stuff the bristles into") were next to the spare hoses, and they were next to the stationery because that's what could fit there. Dan had all that in his mind and in a notebook I couldn't decipher even if I could have found it (it was kept with the extra stove alcohol and the extra radar reflector and the extra shoelaces). When I didn't remember where it was I saw distress and panic in his eyes.

On the dock we saw Galápagos lizards sunning. We hitchhiked along a dirt road and rode in the back of a pick-up truck, with vegetables, to the little town of Bella-Vista and climbed to the top of the island's highest peak. Dan romped up, goat-style; I slowly counted off the last seven hundred trudgy steps through the scruffy pasture growth. There are leg muscles you don't use on a boat—in fact I hardly ever use them except when I'm on that heart-stress treadmill every two years. In a small ocean boat your body is constantly and instinctively shifting to adapt to the lively motion, so your muscle tone is good and you're tuned, but you don't walk much, and your wind isn't kept up. We napped at the top of the peak, peered into the overgrown crater, and saw *Sparrow* seven miles off in the harbor. Horses came to us. On the way down, big cows, apparently beautiful specimens, scared me. Dan knows about animals; he went to a school that had a farm. He and another boy raised a pig and slaughtered it, but their friends deserted them at the critical moment and, only two, they couldn't lift it immediately after death into the boiling water, which loosens the bristles. And that summer we ate the sectioned pork, and we had to trim off the hair when it was on our plates. It was a so-so sharing experience.

We had dinner at a small hotel with the owners, two men who searched the world for paradise and found it here, they told us once too often. It's not the island: that was fine—a nice place, good climate, no storms; it was just the search for paradise that seemed phoney to Dan and me. We figured that paradise has to be a side effect of other searches.

The next day we did some shopping for a few last bits and pieces of hardware, bought shirts that seemed wonderful but that we knew we'd never wear, and went to the weekly movie, *Blade Runner*. It was in English, or so I thought—mostly grunts and never a complete sentence, and the sound quality was awful anyway. The subtitles were in Spanish. The reels were shown in the wrong order. Dan had seen it a few times and tried explaining it, which didn't help me. The crowd was merry. The whole town seemed to show up.

I won another million the next day because there was a pizza place in town.

"Look, Dan, look at that sign—you owe me another million—it says PIZZA."

"Where? I don't see it. Anyway, that's not the right spelling."

So we went in and had some. Not bad. Primitive pies made by the pizza-naïve can be good, and pizza made by experts can be wonderful. It's the in-between—badly crusted and lukewarm—that is irritating. But this was hot, and we both had the obligatory bits of burnt-off skin on the roofs of our mouths. I remembered a conversation with my mother. "Come on, Mom, have a slice, just so you can say you ate pizza." "My dear David," said this Victorian lady, who could roll her R's, "the subject Rarely Arises."

When we made the spare for our friend's self-steerer, he was grateful and wanted to do something in return. "Give us a breakfast," I said, and we had it, on board their boat, with real bacon—no hair on it—served by the pretty lady of the boat. Dan moans about being horny all the time, but I was willing to settle for that moment, sharing a delicious meal and the intelligent companionship of a lovely woman. Boy, you need time to appreciate life, I told him. He just grunted. At his age the only women that look good are between sixteen and twenty. At my age they look good between sixteen and fifty, and counting. It's a genuine glory of maturity ("maturity"—a word I've never thought of using).

After breakfast we cast off for Easter Island. We waited until eight. All of our papers were cleared, and we had managed a week in the islands despite the rule. But if we'd wanted to leave before the customs man's day began, at eight, he had said we'd have to pay his overtime. We knew he wouldn't be there at eight either, but we were deterred from leaving early by the thought of some terrified Ecuadoran recruit firing at us with the ancient machine gun on the bow of that gunboat. That was a mistake, because in the light winds we couldn't make it to our planned overnight in Post Office Bay at Santa Maria, a small south-lying island. On that shore was a barrel with name boards of famous vessels that stopped there in whaling days. Mail was put in the barrel in the hope that a homeward-bound ship would pick it up. It's a shrine for mariners, and we wanted to see it. Dan had carefully burned "Sparrow" on a small teak board. Night fell as we were attempting the poorly marked entrance, so we gave up, stood off, and took our departure for Easter Island. Perhaps no great loss, because we had learned the day before that the Ecuadoran Navy had cleaned up the area and thrown away the signs.

"We'll give our name board to The Horn," said Dan. The light was soft in the dusk.

We went below where Dan cooked his best dish, green noodles with garlic, onions, canned clams, tamari sauce, and grated cheese. We ate, the small table was between us, and then I leaned back on the settee.

"Dad, stop staring at me." Not realizing I was doing so, I had been staring at him. We sat so close to each other, across the narrow cabin table; when I relaxed, my gaze would settle on this person, so easy to look at, whom I love. He was always a handsome child and an eager and curious companion. He always possessed and shared the treasure of self-awareness: in the car, at five years old, "Dad, are we closer?" A moment's pause, then, "Good grief, Dad, what a stupid question!"

At ten, he ordered "see fish, see through clothing" glasses by mail. They didn't work. "You know, Dad, I suddenly realize why they said 'small size only' in the comic book. No one with a full-size head would be stupid enough to order these."

We had spent joyful times together building the interior of the catboat, and later a house, but it was not so happy, earlier, with our elaborate model railroad. I was too aggressive, and he was a sullen partner. At six he loved the one lighted engine on the one loop of track, but not the cranes and switching yards that proliferated too fast. Instead, he helped his friends build their systems, with skills I didn't realize he'd learned.

We built our island house together when he was sixteen, and he worked furiously. He'd been thrown out of boarding school the winter before for defiance of simple rules—attention-getting campus heroics with liquor runs, drugs, a mooning in the dining hall; he'd done everything but study. And his famous satin sheets. He ordered those by mail too, and they worked. I drove up to Vermont to bring him home at the start of the Christmas break. I phoned from Springfield, halfway home, and learned the decision of the faculty meeting that afternoon. The principal said, "No way, David, the faculty doesn't want him back." "Can I drive back up and talk to you, Tom?" He owed us the meeting; Dan, after all, had turned himself in to exonerate a wrongly accused boy.

Dan and I drove back to the school together. "Dan, I know about the flag pulled down to half-mast by your student fans—you've made yourself a hero. Sure, the faculty, every last one of them and Tom too, are all assholes. Now you're out. Don't keep telling me how stupid they all are. Really, Dan, deep in your heart, do you want to continue there if you could?"

There was a long pause. It had started to rain. I still

remember the swish of the wipers. I had a flash of another session on the carpet, three years before—and a funny one. Leonora and I and Dan and another headmaster. Dan had worked the spotlight at assembly, and turning the color wheel to green on the headmaster was the last straw. We were in his office. No longer a brilliant green, just pale and tired, he was droning from a long typewritten list. Nothing seemed that inventive, but the list was remarkably long: "Ink on Becky Cohen's braids, hanging by your knees from the fire escape, mice in Mr. Hamilton's desk drawer, Saran Wrap on the faculty toilet seats, swinging between the buildings on a rope, chewing gum stuck on the elevator button, ringing the fire bell during PTO meeting . . ." On and on. When he finished the list the principal looked up at Dan over his half-glasses. A pause, then a small voice from the small boy, "The mice in Mr. Hamilton's desk was a long time ago."

I stopped the car at a diner and we ran in through the rain. Over coffee Dan said, "Yes, Dad, I want to go back."

At the principal's house Dan chose to wait in the car. I went in and sat with Tom. I remember hooked rugs. Tom explained that what the faculty feared was not Dan's grades—he'd get by—but his after-hours showing off. "It's the way he can blow fire, five feet of flame, and the matches zipping in through windows of the wooden buildings—he really will burn us down."

I said, in the fashion of the popular film of the day, "Tom, I'll make you an offer you can't refuse. We'll move to Vermont and he'll live with us off campus. We'll rent a house. He'll be a day student."

We did that. We rented a charming shack with a wood stove, an improved woodshed. Leonora flew up on weekends. Dan wasn't pleased. He had a double dose to swallow. His pride and now even his independent contrition were compromised. Again, I'd horned in on his life.

"All my hobbies, too, Dad," he said. "I start 'em, like

bird-watching, then you pick 'em up and stifle me. If I were gay you'd become president of 'International Dads of Gays' and wreck even that for me."

It wasn't easy for me. I was lecturing at a college and the daily commute to work could be three-cornered: Putney, Cambridge, New London, Putney. The psychiatrist (Dan had to pledge an hour a week for counseling) was displeased. "Best let it all fall apart and make him start from scratch. This is a bad repair." But Dan was taken back the next fall as a boarding student, and he graduated. I said, "Tom, can we graduate him early, like a secret wedding? It's six hours until the big ceremony and I hate to risk it."

That was the summer, after the long commute, that we built a house on a few rocks in the mouth of the Thames River. Dan worked hard from first light to dark. We didn't talk much about the past semester. I wasn't ready to tell him that it had been the most joyful spring of my life — six to eight hours' driving a day had been a small price to pay for being of real use. Dan wasn't sure whose drama took first place. But we worked and we laughed. "Dad, can you believe this? Look — I'm standing on this board I'm trying to lift!" And we clowned like the silent-film comics who pick up a plank, turn around with it and knock their helper flat, and then turn around to see what they've done and knock him flat again just as he stands up.

Yes, he had been a handsome child, and so eager — always smiling. Then, at six, the steady smile stopped, except for a grimace when a photo was taken. He went inward and struggled. He and his sister fought often in the mornings, but went to school hand in hand, she a bright cheerful scholar, bounding down the sidewalk, and he dragging his steps to the bus stop, dreading another day as class butt. Through the years when I parted from Julia, I was happy at what she was doing; leaving Dan, I always had a lump in my throat. Was he happy? I loved them equally, and raced to meet them with my heart pounding like a lover, but he, never she, was the prodigal.

When Julia left for college, loneliness overwhelmed him. One week he worked feverishly toward a test, declaring, "I'm tired of being last in the class—I'm going to be best." And he made the only perfect score on the weekly test. But his teacher, in her wisdom, changed the 100 to a 0, because he'd written the answers in pen, not pencil. Another gateway shut by the stupid, the pompous.

When I mentioned this during the voyage, he said, "Imagine—if I'd gotten the 100, I'd be sitting here in a three-piece suit."

I looked over at him in the lamplight, across *Sparrow*'s table, and then I couldn't look because my eyes shut hard against a picture. I hit him when he was a child, not once but three different times.

"Sure, hit, hit, hit an eleven-year-old . . ." I told him, years later, horrified at myself. He let it sit, but when I said it again in a year, he told me it was all right, he knew how provocative he was. I said that wasn't enough, I had too many nightmares, too much agony over what I'd done, and he squared around and hugged me hard enough to make me gasp, and said he loved me, he understood, and please not to be troubled anymore.

He was often cool and removed as a youngster. But one afternoon I took a nap (those were days when I often worked through the night at my drafting table) and Leonora joined me. I wasn't asleep when the door quietly opened and Dan came in. I watched through almost closed eyes. Dan looked at us and gently drew up a blanket to cover us. His lips were pressed together hard to prevent a smile.

When Dan was fifteen, Mack Scism, a dear friend to us both, said that Dan had the European tragic sense of life. He didn't mean tragic boohoo, but tragic in the sense of the curve between birth and death. At fifteen. Yes, Mack was right.

We found a big orange rubber buoy at sea on our voyage north in the catboat, and for two years we pummeled each other with it. If you opened a door, there it was flying at you on a rope, a huge silent pendulum whomping you, three steps into the room. Before we went to sea this time, Dan had been working on a way to slip it under my mattress and have it suddenly inflate by gas cylinder.

The wrapped zucchini was his greatest success. I had invited a friend, Hal Lorin, to our island; on the way out I pulled our lobster pots and two lobsters, then stopped at our tiny island garden and picked a fine zucchini and made a delicious lunch. The next week I invited Jack Evans, the chairman of my board. I told Dan of my pride in the home-caught, home-grown lunch, and said that the one remaining zucchini would be ripe and perfect. All started well. The pot came up with two lobsters. They were truly my catch, although I had planted them in that pot before Jack arrived. We walked from the dock, up the path, and I said, "Jack, I've grown a great zucchini for us. Look here." I reached into the bush where it was growing and what I pulled out was a green cardboard supermarket produce tray, Saran-Wrapped and complete with a price sticker, the zucchini inside.

If this all sounds like male-bonding rituals, well, we've tried those too. We went fire-walking when Dan was twenty. It was his idea. We went to a hippie workshop in New Paltz, New York. About thirty of us built a fire, and then introduced ourselves to each other, telling our motivations. One macho fellow said, "I've always lived close to the razor's edge . . ." I said I wanted to do it because Dan wanted to. When the fire was raked to coals, we walked across, barefoot. The macho man was first, walking with that ridiculous "my-balls-are-so-big-I-have-to-walk-bowlegged" gait. He was followed by a thin pale girl of fifteen or so. We were told to keep an image in our minds as we walked. Dan preceded me. He was my image.

Dan, Dan. Now my captain and companion. Leonora said to me that I was selfish to delay his getting on with his life so that I could make my own dream voyage. Well, maybe. But maybe we shared it. At one point in the voyage, I don't remember when, Dan and I discovered that we at least share an image. We both imagine we are alone together, and our little ship has gone down in just seconds. We have failed to extricate and trip open the life raft. We're dog-paddling in the water—no life preservers, nothing but water for a thousand miles. We paddle close. There's nothing but doom for us, no way out. And so we joke. "Hey, Dad, look at me!" "Betcha can't do this, Dan." That would be the way of it.

Fortunately, we also share a life spent learning to keep such moments from happening. Sailing goes far back with us—I first took Dan out when he was three, and by ten he was telling me how to do it better. He was usually right. Once after a supper party on our island, Dan brought us in on the launch and helped a frail lady ashore. He stepped back on board and swung down into the body of the boat. "Oh my, my!" she cried. "He's in his *element!*" And he was indeed. It's as if, however well I sail, I'll always have an accent, because I didn't stand on a deck until I was nine, on my father's boat. It's Dan's native language.

In the little cabin of *Sparrow* are two photographs I had reduced to fit small frames for the tiny space. One is of my father, the other is of the schooner *Sunbeam*, on which I spent my summers growing up. We were never rich people, but certainly well off, because my father was a professional man and didn't lose his money in the Depression. His cousin Ed Nathan had a small sailboat, and after a weekend sail Dad impulsively went into partnership with

Ed on the sixty-foot Alden-designed vessel. Somehow Dad didn't anticipate that my mother would insist on coming aboard. Ed bowed out after the first summer. We would move on board after school, in early June, and we'd come ashore after Labor Day. Our paid captain, Carl Lisberg, was Oslo born, and when Dad returned to work in New York during the summer, Carl could keep us safe. We would moor in a busy harbor such as New London, Newport, Nantucket, or Marblehead, and Dad would go into "the City" for a week or two. In some of these harbors my brother and I made friends and we'd play on the water, rowing or sailing the dinghy *Moonbeam* as if possessed, exploring beaches, going to movies, or playing board games when it rained. We did hours of work each day on *Sunbeam*, and under Carl's sharp eye the work was never tedious. It seemed noble to us—the tradition of the sea and all that.

I remember Carl as always tanned, a well-built man with a broken-nosed face that said "sea dog" to me. He loved black coffee, and when he held his cup high, I suspected there was something else in the coffee he didn't want us to smell. He had bad teeth, wonderfully keen eyes, and represented to me the sea warrior in the way kids of my time thought of Indian braves. He sang Norwegian songs and taught me a few, and when I sang one years later to stagehands in Oslo, they blushed. Carl had been crew on one of the great cup defenders, the J-boat *Enterprise*, skippered by Harold Vanderbilt. He wanted the *Sunbeam* to be perfect and beautiful, and probably was teased by his colleagues about our tobacco-brown sail covers. Every year he asked my father to change them to white. Carl began to drink heavily during his shipyard work during the war, and afterwards he never really made it back with us. On the way home from the Bermuda race in 1946 he lay drunk for two days in the bilge, curled around the engine. Today, when I heat yesterday's coffee and it boils over, I remember Carl and his favorite aroma.

My father was not a fine sailor. He did not have the instincts for wind or wave motion or sail trimming that my brother, Richard, and I developed, perhaps from our small-boat sailing. He was a good coastal navigator, proud of his precision based on logic and accuracy, and he loved to spot the buoys and lighthouses coming into sight on cue. But none of us was given Dan's true feeling for the ocean. Those prewar years seem now to be all of my growing up, but there were only three before *Sunbeam* went into service. During the Second World War she idled in the Atlantic, off Montauk, ready to report submarines. This was called "Picket Patrol" and perhaps was useful in keeping enemy submarines out of Long Island Sound and other bays and harbors. After the war we sailed her for two years, but the world had changed. My brother was studying during summers, and most of the time *Sunbeam* was in harbor. I replaced Carl, and spent two seasons caring for her—all that teak, all that varnish. Often Dad and I couldn't even find a third person to help us sail her.

Sparrow needs only one, however, and Dan and I are two.

The Galápagos were fun, a good stop, we've become a team. The glories of the fauna and flora somehow escaped us. We saw the famous lizards and birds and seals just in the course of sailing or rowing in the harbors. The huge old turtles in the zoo were like the ones we've seen in other zoos—we didn't go to some of the areas where they live in a more natural state. Like voyagers in a boat, their home surrounds them and that seems their wonder. But after our first real voyage, of only twelve days, we were more interested in our own species. That, plus care of the boat, and thoughts of the trip ahead, filled the days.

But now we were on that trip ahead, and when I

returned to the deck after dinner, during my evening watch, there was a bump. A surprised and suddenly awakened seal looked at me crossly in the moonlight off the stern. We were away to Easter Island, moving well.

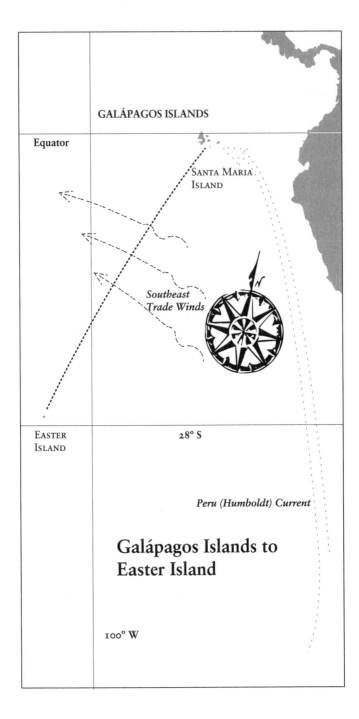

GALÁPAGOS ISLANDS

Equator

SANTA MARIA
ISLAND

Southeast
Trade Winds

N

EASTER
ISLAND

28° S

Peru (Humboldt) Current

Galápagos Islands to Easter Island

100° W

7   THE PERFECT PASSAGE

A great cape, for us, can't be expressed in lon-
gitude and latitude alone. A great cape has a
soul, with very soft, very violent shadows and
colours. A soul as smooth as a child's, as hard
as a criminal's. And that is why we go.

   —*Bernard Moitessier,* The Long Way

DAN

DAY 124. The sea is roly-poly in the early morning, like margarine ripples. A bright scrap of moon is awake with me and so are the stars. The Galápagos are out of sight astern. Two thousand miles ahead is a dot of humanity called Easter Island toward which we go.

It is cold—I have a shirt, sweatshirt, and jacket on, as well as long pants. My special "Cape Horn" hat lies ready, a World War II Russian cap that has wool flaps. Hot coffee and a book full of Robert Louis Stevenson stories await me. Gray clouds darken the sky. The moon grows indistinct, then sleeps.

Here's the daily routine: at 0600 I say, "Dad—it's six," and unceremoniously I get into bed. I sleep heavily and dreamily till about ten. Dad's dozing or reading. I come up on deck and take a sun sight. Depending on how I feel, I'll work it out or go back into my clothy nest to read, fiddle with the radio, or sleep. I'm active again for a noon sight, followed by twenty minutes of fussing to establish our position. Dad comes down to sleep for two hours, and I go

on deck and have my daily ration of soda pop—lately
something called Old Colonial, a grape-ish drink from the
Galápagos. Then I read, write, do odd jobs or avoid them.
I am presently avoiding stowing the inflatable boat. Today
we dumped out four cans of truly awful "protein meal" we
bought in Jamaica. Even Tiger won't taste this. I'm even
afraid to throw it overboard for the fish. We should bury it
at sunrise with a stake through the heart of each morsel.
Around three-thirty I start eating *anything*. Toward five I
start cooking dinner. Tonight we'll have corn—fresh on
the cob—and some salad that's going rotten, and protein
of some sort. After Dad cleans the dishes, I sleep till midnight. My watch, when it comes, is full of reading by the
night light I put in the cockpit. I write and sometimes
sleep—waking on the half-hour to stagger upright and
look about for boats, land, whales, or whatever I was
dreaming about. Sunrise is my favorite time. Alone and
peaceful.

Dear Max and Michelle,
    I wish I had a letter from you to inspire me to write
'cause I feel like a grungy flea . . . Right now we're four
degrees or 240 sea miles south of the equator and
ninety-five degrees west of Greenwich, England, to the
left of Texas and way down. *Sparrow* is moving at six
knots with one reef in the mainsail. The winds are
steady trade winds here. I'm bursting with frustrations
at Dad, who shows signs of oldness and meagerness.
The way that I love him is to get furious 'cause Daddy
has always been God to me and here I am doing stuff
better. This psychological flip is exasperating.
    Last night I woke up to "*Shitfuck!*" which is how
Dad gets himself really angry. Here we are having this
adventure, and booming at five knots, bright starry
sky, and Dad's having a *shitfuck!* fit. I wonder why he
can't have a little patience with whatever inanimate

object he is yelling at. Sometimes he varies it, yelling, "*Fuckshit!*" And I wonder why can't *I* have a little patience with *him*?

A wave just got in my coffee—damn . . . Love, Dan

The cat fell into the pressure cooker, onto the custard I was making. We hardly notice the hairs, except when they lodge in the back of our throats. We could get hairballs.

DAY 128. Six hundred miles from the Galápagos with thirteen hundred to go to Easter Island. Wind is at south-southeast at twenty knots and the seas are five to eight feet and steep. Some breaking. The motion is violent and produces apathy. Even writing is laborious and I must brace my body. I like the chart we are using now—Panama to Cape Horn—all of the west coast of South America and Cape Horn itself. The scale is so big that ten miles can be lost in a dull pencil line. It makes navigation somewhat easy—and seeing that we are so far from anything, a ten-mile error is irrelevant. We have not seen any signs of life—human life—for five days now.

I must describe cooking (for lack of a better word) on board, and Dad (for lack of a better cook) will be the cook. This is, however, a true story—completed just moments ago: I'm off watch, trying to sleep. I hear the sound of cucumbers and tomatoes being sliced—I can tell by the *fwap* or *squish* noises they make when they don't bounce off the cabin floor. Dad asks Tiger, "Do you like tomatoes?" Meanwhile the alcohol preheating the kerosene burner is almost gone so Dad squirts more from our plant mister. Blue explodes, briefly engulfing the stove, ceiling, and the upper half of Dad. *Panic is about* and suddenly I hear, "Oh *fuckshit*—hold this," and an opened can of tuna fish with the oil oozing over the lid is thrust at me. I notice a three-and-a-half-foot trail of oil along the floor with a six-inch clean area where Tiger was lying. The fire has now died out, but the mayonnaise is lost, rolled into the fruit locker perhaps. The smell of burning toast fills the cabin (a few pieces are still on fire), and I experience the sensation of warm tuna oil that has dripped down my arm and is pooling on my pillow next to my elbow. Then, miraculously, the pepper, oregano, and knife are all "lost," having slid or bounced into various nooks and crannies. There is melting butter on the wall near the hatch and there are feline butter-footprints leading forward . . .

Dad's definition of cooking (given to me after I complained of finding a sardine in my camera case) is as follows: "Cooking is time spent in the galley area, after which, the food scraped out of the utensils and off the walls is served."

DAY 129. 0400. I set the clocks back one hour as we cross 97° 50' west. One extra hour in which I dream about girls and bathtubs. The cat is chewing the life preserver.

DAY 131. Today is our Thanksgiving feast. We have all the fixings except cranberry sauce. In New York City (where I lived until I was fourteen) we lived so close to a small grocery store that we didn't have to plan our meals. We sometimes shopped between courses. Here it's different. Dad makes an amazing sauce he calls "*Sparrow* Sauce," which contains raspberry and strawberry preserves, walnuts, raisins, apple, slivers of orange peel, and then horseradish! The horseradish gives it an edge and takes away the sweetness. It's good and we're happy. Tiger eats so much that he passes out on his back.

Later—like a deliberately thrown softball—a flying fish lobs over the dodger with a torrent of spray and plops into the cockpit at my feet. In surprise I laugh out loud. Hearing the flapping, I stop. I turn my flashlight on him; his head is digging into the one small puddle of water in the cockpit created by the boat's heeling. He shakes, gasping, with his wings held open like a Chinese kite, blue paper. I think of him as my breakfast. We've had a few, and they were good. But we found them dead in the morning. I thought briefly of how right it is—even natural—to gather protein from the sea, how insignificant this creature is—so abundant in the ocean that he randomly flew into my boat—out where the word "vast" does not describe—does not even begin to pull the strings of thought into existence of how big the sea is. I let him go. Maybe to atone for past murders, injuries to life, or maybe because I want to later on justify what I will do, as if there were a karma currency. I feel happy.

DAY 133. I woke this morning to a beautiful and powerful vision of big waves. During the night there were many squalls and the seas built to over twelve feet. They are long slow rollers like passionate sex and locomotives. I can see the horizon only for a moment when we balance at the crest—then we slide into a blue valley.

DAY 135. This could just go on forever.

DAY 136. Calm day—we take turns "falling overboard" and getting rescued—we find problems with our quick-release life ring, so now we know and can fix it. Dad tries making candy by frying slices of lime in honey, which doesn't work. Two hundred and twelve miles to go—getting an Easter Island radio station, full of old, scratchy American rock records. Dad polishes brass—amazing to see that he has patience to do that. Old-fashioned sailors love to see shiny things on a ship.

Sunrise looks like a gray calamity. Big swells from the south; tiny Portuguese man-of-war bubbles float past.

DAY 138. I keep imagining the ocean suddenly frozen solid into glass or marble—when it's calmish, so you'd have endless hills and ripples, and what it would feel like under bare feet and under a bicycle tire. It'd be fun to drive a car fast over it.

DAVID

Sure, I was a little queasy the first day and I thought our young hero was too. The first night things fell on me. But *Sparrow* settled quickly into this passage. For some reason that no one has satisfactorily explained, it seems to take a sailing boat some days to ease and stretch and really fly on a voyage. Conrad speaks of this. But now we were moving. I never look at a passage chart for the first few days, even if I'm navigating. I put down the little noon crosses, but fold the chart away quickly because the crosses show such a depressingly meager bite into the big distance to cover. After four or five days you can look and start rationalizing the passage: "Well, we've gone four hundred miles and in only one more day that will be five hundred and that's one-quarter of the passage, and then in another day it will probably be over six hundred and that's one-third, and you're almost halfway," and so on. Every five hundred miles I shaved. Every thousand miles we would toast—a little cup of Tia Maria or Kahlua.

I don't know why it is that when you love to sail you spend your life dreaming of being at sea and then do all you can to speed into your destination harbor. Maybe it's because each leg of the journey is like a little work of art, and you want to press yourself and the boat to the utmost. The practical answer is that the faster you do it, the less exposure there is to bad weather, which no one really likes. But I remember reading a good sailor's description of heaven as being a place with fine boats and beautiful steady winds, and once in a while, God, please send a gale.

For a while, after Joshua Slocum, small-boat voyages became almost a British specialty, often in the Vertue-class sister ships of *Sparrow*, or slightly bigger versions of her, such as *Wanderer III*. I studied for a year in London soon after the Second World War, and my theory is that for the British the cold and damp and bad food on a tiny boat were indistinguishable from home; they didn't realize that they weren't in their living rooms.

Our living rooms at home weren't like this, though — and neither were our bedrooms. On board we had cloths or slings that tied up to the handrails, and these kept us in our berths when she rolled. I preferred to sleep on the port tack (wind coming from our left) and I lay against this cloth sling, hammock-like, suspended with hardly any part of me resting on the berth itself. Dan liked this tack too; his starboard berth was low and as we heeled to starboard, he lay up against the hard back of the settee.

British we weren't, but *Sparrow* was, so we wanted to live up to the tradition, if not the misery. Everything should work: food should be nourishing and reasonably tasty; every screw and bolt perfect; and our way of moving about the boat should be elegant, if you could call it that, as we plunged along. I had expected to be battered and bruised in the course of the voyage, and even thought of bringing along an ice-hockey helmet. (I did have elbow pads, but never used them.) I fell once on the first leg of the voyage and had a bruised butt. Once, I missed the hand grip over my berth and hit my elbow on that electric spot, shooting awful nerve sparks through my arm for an hour. But I soon learned, and getting about below was like a good squash game where the players circled each other in the center of the tiny court, spinning this way and that. Sometimes it was almost beautiful. We drifted about this cabin like weightless astronauts speeded up ten times, with the cat zipping in the other direction. By this time we were rarely in each other's way.

In tight quarters like this, though, it was good that Dan and I didn't mind being physically close. And why shouldn't we be? For years I carried him on my back with his little arms around my neck. Now I sometimes walked down these strange towns with my hand on his shoulder. Of course, I wished he wouldn't still leap into supermarket carts at home and make me wheel him around as we shopped. Once I got back at him by going to the desk and asking for a loudspeaker announcement: "Daniel Hays, your father is at the lost-and-found desk waiting for you." He retaliated by sneaking out and driving away in the car.

Our routine was all-important, and Dan developed it. Usually ships run on some variation of the four-hour watch. With a two-person crew, you alternate—four hours on deck, four below, three times a day. Dan proposed six-hour watches twice a day, and I'd never heard of that. He argued that the off-watch crewman could get close to a full night's sleep, short only a brief nap, and that the Navik would do most of the work and not demand exhausting attention during the spell. Furthermore, virtually all of tiny *Sparrow*'s deck work and sail changing could be done by one man, and the sleep of the man below would be uninterrupted. It would be like two single-handers sailing together. And it was good—it worked. Dan never woke me to help him change sails during our five months, and I woke him only twice—once when I was so tangled in lines because of a crazy maneuver, bound like Gulliver, and he came on deck to steer while I sorted out the foredeck. The other moment was in Drake Passage. Sometimes, when I was frustrated and doing my usual swearing, he poked up his head and told me how he hated to be awakened by profanity. I was reminded that years ago, Leonora took a self-development course but continued to smoke. Dan, even at eleven, hated to see that self-destruction, and one night complained at supper. "My son," said Leonora with her new assurance, "I smoke. That's the way I am, Dan, that's the real me, and you just have to live with it." Dan thought for a moment, then reached over and snatched the cigarette out of her mouth and dropped it into her glass of wine. She started to yell and he said, calmly, "I just put out your cig-arette in your wine. That's me. That's the way I am, the real me, your son." I tried that line with Dan about my pro-fanity, but it didn't have much success. I had better results turning back another of his old lines. When he instructed me about my various imperfections, I turned my eyes upward and quoted him: "Is this going to be another boring lecture?" It made him furious—he could not find a snappy answer, which served him right, because for over ten years I had never found one.

Only once did I sail with my father for an extended time. After we sold the *Sunbeam*, we bought a smaller boat, a capable yawl designed by Sparkman and Stephens, but time had run out on our sailing as a family, and Dad couldn't sail her alone, as Dan or I can now sail *Sparrow*. The summer I was nineteen we sailed together for ten days. I brought the boat from Norwalk to Marblehead with a friend, and then Dad and I sailed in the beauties of Casco Bay. I'd looked forward to it for almost a year; plans like this are often made at the conclusion of the season before, a "Why don't we . . ." that is realized once in a great while. But I'd had a gnawing doubt, the doubt that engaged cou-ples have: would we have enough conversation for all that time, just the two of us? Couples remember it as a silly worry; it wasn't silly for Dad and me. We simply didn't have the small talk. I don't believe it was painful for Dad. I doubt if he felt the need for more than my presence, which he cherished. Dad could relax, could lie in the sun, be quiet. I could be quiet too, and so can Dan (never mind the sun part: we both regard sunbathing as an unnatural and torturous inactivity, an Olympic event). But I felt a lack, I wanted to talk more; it was not an angel of silence that came on board, it was an awkward division, to me. My father and I had no shared reading, no habit of describing what we were reading, or urging a book on the other, and then arguing about it; we had no music to dispute, no houses that we had built together, no plans involving long-term effort together. Dad and I worked well together, coming into harbor with our division of sailing duties, rowing ashore, shopping. But in between there was no small talk, no spirited disputes about technology.

It never was that way on board *Sparrow*. We always had chatter, a lifetime of shared projects, as much to talk about as an old married couple, and no awe. During this passage to Easter Island, Dan and I installed a small cleat for the foreguy, the line that holds the main boom forward to prevent a jibe at sea. Indeed, arguing about whether to call it a foreguy or a preventer took up half of one day. We drilled two holes through the fiberglass cockpit rim and through a plywood back-up plate, and then Dan crawled below into the cockpit locker. That was not easy; the locker had to be half emptied and even then the squirming took five full minutes. I put on the bedding compound and pushed through the bolts, Dan put more compound on the nuts and held them while I turned the bolts. Done, and a good job, while the boat gyrated like a kite without a tail and we shouted instructions over the noisy sea. When I pulled Dan out by his ankles, we laughed about the difficulties and we were proud.

My father could barely change bait on a fishhook. He loved to prune trees and shrubs, and he did have one mechanical skill—hanging pictures. He could hammer in the nail and adjust the height by re-twisting the picture wire. But we never shared toy trains, and he never hung on to a nut while I turned the bolt.

There is another part of this history, of course. Our Connecticut home was on a pond, and when I was home and the weather favored us, my father and I would put in our small canoe and paddle for an evening half-hour. We followed the same route, which we loved, and in that repetition saw the beautiful and subtle changes of the seasons. We were always silent, an Indian kind of silence in the light boat on the still water was our pleasure. I'm now sure Dad felt that same quietness, that silent pleasure on our cruise, but it hurt me, then.

And yet, I realize that the voice that comes to me now, his voice, belongs to that one cruise; it is the sound of his voice when we did speak between those silences. I hear the "Steady, boy," or "Hold on," the "Be a little more patient," and even the mild annoyance that he expressed about something I was doing badly, when he said, "Yuy, yuy, yuy" (accent on the first "yuy," and not pronounced to rhyme with "oy" as in "toy," but the lower "u" as in "rut"). I hear that often, and the voice comes from those ten days. It's as if the rest of our life together was a silent movie, fully understood, as if captioned, but with the actual resonance, the timbre of my father's voice, placed in that short soundtrack, spliced in.

My favorite part of the day's routine was the time Dan and I spent together in the afternoon. *Sparrow* steered herself—closely supervised of course. As the voyage went on, in these empty unfrequented routes, we spent more and more time below, checking the course on the below-deck compass. Voyages are made *in*, not *on*, ships. At four we stopped our maintenance routines of sewing, checking the radios, going over the day's position figures, and so forth, and we played cards. It was up and down, but I was generally ahead in this long gin contest.

"That's because you cheat, Dad."

"*Me* cheat? That, from the boy who always took one piece from the jigsaw puzzle to drive us crazy?"

"I always put it back."

"Sure, after we looked under the sofas and the chairs, rolled up the rug . . ."

"Well, it made a kind of dramatic finish to each puzzle."

"And the Monopoly money in your shoe!"

"Dad, it hurts me that you say that. I've known you all my life."

With cards we had our classical music cassette concert.

Dan feigned annoyance, but I knew that he listened to this kind of music when I wasn't around. Sometimes we played an opera, and to Dan there was just one plot—"Boy meets girl, his friend sells an overcoat, and she jumps off the castle wall yelling 'Aiuto.'" I accepted that. He needed his music for many hours each day; I was content with mine for a good hour or two. He had the kindness to use his earphones. I made up verses for him. "Heeah I is, with my geetah sticking straight up in front o' me, pointing dayown thet long, long road sticking out in front o' me, hump, hump, hump," or "I'm fourteen and haven't had (hump, hump) for two days, this Mama's life is over . . ."

"Dan, did I ever tell you about . . ."

"Yes, Dad, *many* times."

I could try numbers for my thoughts. "Seventy-four, Dan."

"No, Dad, sixteen." He also knew my train of thought and could pick it up, like Sherlock Holmes, as it went down the track, five minutes after some small event set it in motion.

At five we started to cook. I didn't have much patience cooking the big meal when the boat leapt about, so I did the chopping, on a little cutting board, while sitting on my berth. I'm not as good a cook as Dan. I chopped garlic, onions, cabbage, and fresh vegetables as long as they lasted. The point of our cooking was to use as few pots and utensils as possible and produce something good that could be eaten with chopsticks from small bowls held in our laps—or else the diners and the whole cabin were decorated with food. A rice base was good. When the rice was cooked he moved it to the perimeter of the pot to stay warm and other foods could be placed in the small and intensely hot center area and then moved aside into the rice as they were done. Dan was inventive but sometimes he panicked too early and it was "save-the-meal time!" and in went the tamari sauce. We worked on the continuous meal theory: you don't clean off your plate and utensils between bites, therefore between meals is only a logical extension of that time. We did wipe things off thoroughly ("Anyone can wash a dish, Dad, but it takes a real man to *wipe* it clean"), and we leaned over the side to swish out the pot and the bowls. That was my job on the six-to-midnight watch, just after supper. (Leaning over that way is how I lost our biggest flying fish, a foot long, which could have been a big lunch. Just as I opened it with our sharp knife a wave thumped down on my back. I saved myself and the knife.)

Another clean-up job on my watch was to clear the cockpit lines of bits of food that I had thrown out during the chopping. Landing those pieces in the ocean could be a hard shot, even for a good waste-basketball executive, because I sat facing starboard with the hatch on my right and Dan working at the stove in between. I had to shoot with my right hand, or an across-the-body shot with my left. The food sometimes hit the hatch inside, or Dan ("It's ready, Dad, it stuck to me"), and if it got through, it might grace the main sheet or the safety lines that bordered the deck. One large petal of onion skin blew forward in a following wind just before Christmas and decorated the bow pulpit until New Year's, frail and luminous. We watched it and were sorry when it washed off. As Dan said, there wasn't much entertainment out there.

There was fresh food, though, and it kept well. Our fresh foods were potatoes and yams, garlic (a bit of which makes anything taste fresh), and onions, as well as oranges and limes and grapefruits that kept for entire passages. We wrapped them loosely in newspaper and stowed them in the forward vegetable bin that we built in Panama. Cabbage also kept—lettuce didn't, perhaps because its leaves were more loosely wrapped. Eggs stayed fresh because we bought them before they could be refrigerated and greased them with petroleum jelly. We preferred this to the other

usual method of keeping them—which is to dip them into
boiling water for a few seconds to hard-boil a few millime-
ters of the white just under the shell—because they were
less likely to crack. Filling your palm with petroleum jelly
and rubbing each egg also used less time and stove fuel.
Rice, of course, was boxed, but we kept it in a plastic tube
intended to hold rolled-up charts. We tried to buy lettuce
and other fresh vegetables and fruits before they were
refrigerated. We would feast on these for the first ten days,
until they spoiled. We bought round, green bananas—if
the ribs showed they tended not to ripen as well. The
bananas ripened all at once, of course, so we would have
three-day banana-eating contests—very sickening. We carried fifty-four gallons of water in our tanks, which was a
lavish supply, and additional plastic bottles of spring water,
some of which we kept in an abandon-ship bag in the
quarter berth. This bag was always ready to be grabbed if
we were sinking and getting ready to launch our automatic
blow-up sea raft, which was different from our inflatable
rowing dinghy. Also in that grab bag were fishing gear,
bright airplane-visible dye, some medications, and an emergency signal beacon that broadcasts on a frequency that
the United States and Russia monitor by satellite.

Sparrow plunged along. It was rough, rough going in
those beam seas, which rolled her more sharply than a following sea. But beam winds moved her well and the
steering was steadier than in following seas. Even on these
plunging nights the little cabin was comfortable and
secure. I sat reading, the oil lamp over my right shoulder.
("Your lamp to the left," my mother always said, and I still
couldn't settle in without hearing a dim and fleeting echo of
her, "You'll ruin your eyes.") The lamp swung in short arcs
and the shadows moved slightly and animated the room.
At the end of each page I glanced at the cabin compass by
my left foot. The numbered circle swung back and forth in
its own small consistent arc. Dan would be asleep, three

feet from me, almost totally out of sight, snuggled deeply into his sleeping bag with Tiger on his forehead. The canvas sling, lashed to the handrail above him, bordered his webby nest—one that moved as the boat heeled from far to farther and back. Dan's navigation books, his radio, cassette player, and earphones, the clocks, barometer, barograph, journals, pens, and his flashlight were all within reach should he sit up. The alarms of his wristwatches "meeped" together in the night, and he would turn in the bunk. Seemingly without waking, Tiger would lift slightly and settle back on his head.

My cup of chocolate would be wedged into the corner of the fence that rims the stove, which also swung with the lamp and the shadows. Forward, in the peak of the boat, a string hammock that held rolls of paper towels, spare line, and the spare paddle to the Navik would also be moving, barely seen except as its extended shadow, and the whole side of the boat seemed to breathe as we moved. It was never quiet, but the whooshes, the thumps, and even the thuds were mellow. A whistle or a shriek of wind pulled me only slightly up from the text, but the jarring strong slaps of waves would make me look up.

When I was on watch I would keep a pipe alive, barely, because the cabin was too small for strong smoke. Every twenty pages, about twenty minutes, I would open the cabin doors, lean out and take a real puff, and then crawl up and out into the cockpit and look slowly around the sky, around again at the horizon, and then I studied the wake for a moment to judge our speed. Every hour I wrote notes in the log. Fifteen minutes before midnight I would start the stove, brush my teeth during the preheat cycle, pump eight strokes of water into the kettle and put it on, cheat ahead with the midnight log entry, tie up my bunk sling, take off outer clothing, and snuggle into my sleeping bag. At midnight, when the kettle whistled, I would wake and say, "Your watch, Dan." He would say, "Hmph," and the cat would stretch and yawn and step on Dan's eyelids on the way down to his bowl.

I say the voyage was perfect because of our fine weather and speed. We covered two thousand miles in under sixteen days and in that time there was a one-thousand-mile week, which is rare in a boat this small. You could easily beat *Sparrow* on Long Island Sound, but at sea she routinely carried sail at her maximum hull speed when other boats would have had to shorten sail and reduce speed to avoid pounding or tumbling over. *Sparrow* moved like a fine big boat. She didn't dive or squat or pound, but entered the waves smoothly. In these side seas, of course, she would from time to time drop off a wave or be smacked by one—a sensation like slamming onto concrete—but all boats do that. When we reviewed this leg in harbor we found that we went true as a dart. Based on our noon positions and great circle calculations we wasted fewer than sixty miles in this flight.

DAN

DAY 139. November 30. The usual tension and excitement before landfall. A shooting star, its bright streaks break into pieces toward the glowing horizon where the sun will rise. I see white trails of smoke in the sky where it was. I smile at the beauty and then just under the smoke I see two lumps—Easter Island.

I wake up Dad and we both look at the very top of an Everest-sized mountain, rising two miles from its base on the cold, dark ocean floor. Seen from the sea, it is smooth, velvety dark green, and massive, rising up to its volcanic peaks. This rock is farther from any other place in the world than any other place is—it is the most isolated land on earth. If you look at a globe of the earth, chances are you won't find it because the printer usually uses this largest vacant area for the name of the company, legend, and such. The closest neighbor is Pitcairn Island, eleven hundred miles to the west. That even smaller island was where Mr. Christian shipwrecked himself and crew after their mutiny on the HMS *Bounty*. I like the neighborhood.

Easter Island is triangular, seven by fourteen by eight miles. Each corner is full of an extinct volcano that holds collected rainwater in small lakes. The island is dry and harsh—the coasts are rough lava, high and precipitous. About three thousand people live here now. A while ago, some of their ancestors carved figures out of the lava, which are still scattered about and cause much excitement to tourists.

The island has a great history—the most isolated place on earth was doing fine until guess who stopped by for a visit. In the name of white rice and virginity, Western man spent a good two hundred years raping, robbing, and leaving neat diseases here. Legend says that there's a wide stone path leading from the island into the sea and on toward Atlantis.

0730. First fly on board. With the wind coming straight across *Sparrow*'s side, we sailed a beautiful beam reach along the coast. The cliffs are sharp and steep—you could literally sail along and touch the cliffs. The sun is bright and the sky very blue.

We anchor off the red-roofed town of Hanga Roa—the only town. We have a shot of Tia Maria and then sleep deeply for two hours. Voices wake us. Four officials (police, customs, army, and doctor) come on board, from a longboat powered by a Japanese outboard. An ancient man, who at one time surely played in a dugout canoe powered only by a paddle, is the driver. They are friendly and through a sort of sign language we are cleared. They tell us where to anchor—closer to town—and explain how to row our dinghy between the rock and the surf to come into the small landing, which is a pocket on the shore, smaller than a basketball court and only a little deeper than a bathtub.

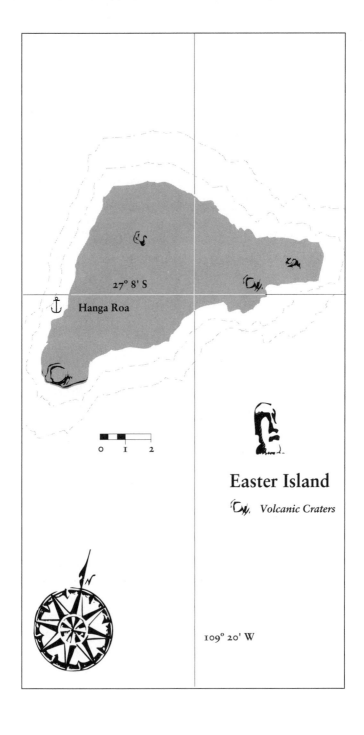

27° 8' S

⚓ Hanga Roa

0   1   2

Easter Island

Volcanic Craters

109° 20' W

8   EASTER ISLAND

From the bottom of my heart I thanked the
boat, I talked to her with endearments that
fled down the howling wind—
     —Vito Dumas, "Alone Through
        the Roaring Forties"

DAN

DAY 140. Adventures with the anchor. It is snagged under huge chunks of boat wreck and concrete slabs that lie in 35 feet of water. I free the chain in two dives and we move and anchor again. Very rocky: on this bottom there are boulders as big as *Sparrow*. We put down the Herreshoff hook, an anchor (especially good for rocks) like the painted ones you see on lawns, and all 160 feet of chain, so I feel safe. The water is cold with 80-foot visibility—not Bahama-bright but steel blue. *Sparrow* looks like a big toe from underwater. Checking the depth with the sounding line, I tantalize a small octopus with the lead weight and he clings to it. Chopped up and tenderized (pounded), he or she is great on our spaghetti dinner.

Dear Max and Michelle,

I've been on the boat so long that going ashore is like Mars. If I get within fifty feet of a beautiful girl I drool, trip, and walk into a tree.

I haven't explored the island yet—we got here a few hours ago and will go ashore in the morning. The famous stone faces you see pictures of are within binocular range. But as yet they are still images in my mind taken from pictures . . . Dad and I are all goose bumps looking at this—we just read *Aku Aku* by Thor Heyerdahl and are living in the mysteries of secret caves and skeletons. The shore is open and

129

exposed to north through southwest winds and no matter which way it blows, the surge is enough to knock a hot coffee cup into your lap.

(Next day.) Going ashore is an adventure: there is a narrow range and a sort of channel where the waves are a little less humongous. If you are too far to one or the other side your rubber raft gets flipped by ocean-size waves.

Again, a main street along the seafront, two going inland, a cross street, a few groceries, souvenir shops, three restaurants. The phone building is modern with a satellite scoop surrounded by a chicken-wire fence.

Cape Horn will be next, and the thought of that excites and scares me. I have no concept of dying, but it is true that few other boats this small have made the passage. Here I am on this earth and I'm going to sail over the roughest part of it! There is a great beauty in powerful weather. I have come to love huge waves and spray blown off the top. I spend hours watching the sun rise over them. Love, Dan

DAY 144. Busy days full of work and food shopping. Dad's made a net to keep the sails all in one place when they're bagged below. He's great like that, he always has at least six projects going on and whatever he gets near gets better. Until now the sails were just falling off the forward bunk, and, with the motion, working their way aft along the floor. They bury the toilet, which is bad if you're sitting on it.

Today, Mom flies in and we go to the airport along with most of the island's population. The pizza man is the customs agent; the guy who rents out horses waves the flashlights at the parking plane. Only two flights land each week (Santiago to Tahiti, and return), so it's a big deal. Mom's luggage has gotten itself to St. Louis.

Moms, what a thing. You start out inside them so helpless they breathe for you. You come out and they do practically nothing else but love you so much that the rest of your life seems like hard work. This mom comes bounding off the plane with the instinct gear set at high, immediately tucking in my shirt. As usual I'm a little embarrassed as she introduces me to half the people on the plane as "the most beautiful child ever." I'm eight years old, again.

DAY 145. A beautiful young woman invites me to go exploring on the island. When I first saw her I had a thought like, "Why is it I never can have 'that kind' of woman? She's so perfect, intangible . . ." Her name is Elizabeth and her eyes are dark and deep, sending ripples of lust through me. We play all day—in caves with human bones in them, in groves of trees that conceal bathtub-sized swimming holes, and on cliffs with ocean crashing below. I invite her to *Sparrow* for dinner. We row out in the dinghy and after ten minutes she is seasick so we head back in.

Why *then*, I don't know, but as we're rowing in, a great big wave breaks on top of us and we are thrown out into the surf. I see the raft escape from under the wave and shoot ten feet up in the air like a pinched watermelon seed. Liz is scared and clings to me. I cling back. Naturally most of Hanga Roa just happens to be standing on the beach so any chance of merely complete embarrassment is blown away. Her shoes are gone. We walk back toward her home laughing, whereupon I meet her dad, who also laughs when Liz tells him about the swim. I love making a good impression on a girl's dad . . .

DAY 146. Mom, Dad, and I rent a Jeep—visit cliffs, huge craters. Boy, you want upsets? Hang out with your parents. A certain tone of voice and a switch is flipped, triggering a string of memories about some anger. It's like being a computer, activated by sound, which sends eight discs spinning and the screen fuzzes. They have an argument. I don't really hear it but I'm sure it's about me. Mom mentions wanting wine or a cigarette and I get so angry—I watch her slowly killing herself, and all I can do is lash out to try and hurt her back. On a beach I rub all the sand off her feet, carefully between her toes, and put on her socks and then her sneakers. I feel such love in serving her, but I do it just once, and how does a mother do that for so many years? She lives her child's life.

I climb all over the huge Easter Island stone heads. I dangle my feet in their eyelashes and am pissed at the guide who yells at me from a great distance. I think, "This is *my* time, you don't get to intrude into my life," and he shuts up. I strip for a photo of me on a giant carving—I want to feel it with all of me. I slide down the nose of an unfinished one that would have been eighty feet long. I climb straight up a cliff over more noses, eyes, lips, chests, and navels. Two statues even have boobs! A whole side of a mountain with figures in all stages of completion, carved at whichever angle worked best with the grain of the rocks. It looks like everyone quit during lunch one day. What beautiful passion and expression—carving on a mountain in almost-forever stone. At least these were too big for Thor Heyerdahl to grab—he took so many of the smaller wooden carvings with him that today there are only two in the island's museum. Chile has only four pieces. Hooray for anthropology.

DAY 149. Liz and I take off on two sluggish horses I call "Trigger" and "Silver." I keep telling them to be enthusiastic, but end up whacking them with a big stick. Elizabeth wears tight pink pants and after five months on a boat, or with just Dad, I . . . well, they are just great pants. We ride to some of the moai (statues) and to strangely pronounced places. Then at a stone beach by Vinapu, we sit in a pool of rounded ocean-soft stones with waves swelling in every few minutes. We sit, watching two snails crawl a few feet, pour water on each other, and then finally when I give up, sure I could never reach over and "risk" everything, *she* reaches out and kisses me. We make ripples in the salt water. I devour her and again later in a clump of ancient trees between volcanoes.

She says, "Poor boy, been on yacht *so* long."

DAVID

Not long after we arrived, I met a pretty girl at the hotel. She said that maybe we could all rent horses and go riding. "Tomorrow's my day off," she said.

"Wonderful," I said. "We can rent an extra horse and take it to meet my wife at the airport, she's coming in tomorrow."

"Wait," she said, "I just remembered that it's the *next* day that I'm free." So she and Dan went off somewhere.

We had phoned Leonora when we first came ashore and left a message on her answering machine. Somehow we hadn't thought of this as a meeting place, but we decided that she had to see this island. She made it happen, via Santiago. I reserved a room in the island's only fancy hotel, a motel layout, and a mistake because some of the guest houses were nicer. But there was a pool and her exercise was swimming. At this season there were only three couples registered, and in his wisdom the manager put us in three adjoining rooms out of the sixty. "Well, Dad, you and Mom will be making a lot of noise—once anyway, har, har."

Leonora arrived with her lists. I wrote sixty postcards to everyone I thought I knew, and she produced a list of eighty-six more, mostly people I realized I wouldn't want to forget, but every time I said, "Do we need that name?" she reminded me of a kindness and I was ashamed. I grew up in comfortable circumstances, as we say; Leonora grew up in Harlem without a father's presence and she struggled, starting work at fourteen, and I became the reticent loner and she loved the world. We started our visit in Hanga Roa with a party for all of the already close friends she met on the plane from Santiago, and there were a few cards to write to people she adored from her few hours in Chile. Our thirtieth anniversary would take place when I was back at sea. She had gifts to be opened after we sailed, from herself and Julia and Jack.

The scene at the airport was pathetic, lost luggage aside. These good people were stepping directly from the natural lazy South Sea existence into an indolence of tourism. There may have been some years of vigor here, but the sheep farms were desolate now, and the island's supplies came from the mainland. Virtually nothing was made or grown except souvenirs and some pineapples. There was minor fishing. At the airport, the people we'd seen as schoolchildren or teachers or fishermen were dressed in badly made hula skirts and costumes that they thought characterized the South Seas. A poor imitation of some culture's dance was being done for deplaning passengers. Soon the passengers were whisked off for a short glance and photograph at a nearby moai, and then, back on the plane. This was just a fuel stop. And so the passengers saw Easter Island; the sad thing was that if you've seen a moai or two, you've seen them all. Unless . . . Well, we did sail out here, which took something. And we sat by the moais for hours as the light slowly changed. But life here today is remote from the great stone heads, and the culture may soon be only a jet stop, as well served by postcards. Interactive moais.

Leonora was as excited about this island as we were, and wanted to take home most of it. She bought little carvings of the statues; they're of stone so that's a lot of overweight. We stowed them on *Sparrow*. She's not a great walker or climber (dancers spend their early years suspended in midair and their later years suspended in traction), but we rented a Jeep and bounced around with her cheer and enthusiasm. It wasn't easy to fit her into our rhythm after these months. We could see *Sparrow* from our hotel window. I love Leonora, I love Julia, and Jack was working his way very fast into my center. Now a shadow hung over us, Cape Horn, and Leonora didn't know it. She thought we were going through the Strait of Magellan (not that she had a secure grasp of geography; the few times she mentioned that bad place she called it "Cape Corn"). Leonora has a bold approach to our language, perhaps from her Hungarian ancestry. Sometimes she seems to feel that it's a tightrope that can slow her down, and she prefers to walk out onto thin air. I write down her sayings, such as "It's a ballpoint figure," "They keep a pietà in town," or "They served raw vegetables with a dip, you know, a coup d'état."

"Strait of Magellan" is what we've told her—it's the red herring Dan and I have told our friends and family. Peter Feller, in Florida, suspected it, I learned later, but said nothing. Jack Evans, chairman of my board, suspected also and asked me outright and I lied, which was hard. And then Julia was engaged and there was one more. What idiocy, I found myself thinking, to go out and drown expensively. I was loaded below my emotional lines. But there was more.

"David, now, you're on your time off, and I don't want to upset you, but . . ."

"Who died?"

"A man, one of our dearest. I'm sorry."

I blurted out two names, two men whose health was a constant worry to them.

"David, I'm sorry, don't guess, don't set our friends in order. We don't see him as often. Sudden, unexpected."

My God, Norman.

"I'm sorry, David."

"No, no, now's the time, it's strange, you don't know . . ."

"Don't know what?"

I meant that out there they come to you, you talk to them, living or dead. That's how I sometimes spent the dusk hours on the passage. I spoke to people I loved but didn't even know, like Kathleen Ferrier, the great Welsh contralto. And I could talk to Norman—it wasn't very different out there, between live or dead friends.

"Did you . . . ?"

"Yes, Julia and I went to Boston. We did what one does, and Pat understands—you're away."

Norman Geschwind was my London roommate, inherited from my brother. He was fifty-eight, brilliant, funny, and he could read a play in less than an hour and explain it to you. His neurological studies had been at their height, and he was telling us how our brain works—dazzling insights. There were so many things I wanted to say. Now, I could only say them to twilights at sea.

By Jeep we saw the whole island on two successive day trips, and we peered over high cliffs, into craters, and into the sea. I hate heights, though I can go cheerfully aloft at sea because I'm in control with a full grip on the mast. When I'm on a tall building or cliff I have that desire to throw myself off, which Dan, referring to Sartre, says is because I am given a basic choice, an alternative and easily possible action. That doesn't help, but I am helped by a friend who reviews for *The New Yorker*, who says that when she's high up she doesn't think of jumping off herself but of a few others she'd like to push. This is funny to me and sets fright in perspective.

Thor Heyerdahl's *Aku Aku* speaks eloquently of Easter Island, and his discoveries and theories broke ground. My favorite passage is when he spoke to the mayor-chief (there still was one, and some men had tribal memory) and said in his modern way that it was impossible to move those statues from their carving places to their final locations: why, it would take hundreds of men! Well, said the chief, maybe 200, and he gathered 180 men and a rope and they pulled a statue along. My theory of history is that things happened in the past the way they do now: someone is in a bad mood or has a cold or the curse or leaves for a day to do laundry, and things happen. I'm not a great believer in inevitable tides. The great mystery of Easter Island remains—not how they made these statues, which we know, or how they moved them and raised them, techniques which we can explain in a few ways. The question is why? What was the religion? What was meant? I wonder if it's all that complicated. There are about 360 of these great statues. It's been shown that 10 men can make an average statue in one year. In 36 years about 100 men could have made all of these carvings. That's not a huge workforce. I've worked professionally for 36 years, a reasonable working span, and any impassioned ruler or his favorite art director could order this work and achieve it in one lifetime. It could have been one person's odd vision, and possibly not a mysterious tradition of centuries and generations. Then one day one person died and it all stopped.

After we'd bounced back to town in the Jeep, we ate dinner at a guest house with another couple. The man had a number tattooed on his arm. He didn't want to talk about it, but he didn't choose to cover it at the dinner table. Strange, out here. I didn't press him.

Sailing has never been a social sport for me. When I was young, we loved cruising as a family: the day's sail, a quiet harbor, time ashore in towns that didn't look as much alike as they do today. Harbors were quiet then, in the years just before the war—quiet and often empty. Perhaps we'd see one other yacht in an out-of-the-way nook, a wooden boat, usually unique. As a boy I knew almost all of the larger Long Island Sound boats, the way kids know cars, and could usually recite the boat's name from a sight of the top of her mast. There were wonderful schooners—*Nina*, *Mistress*—and great yawls such as *Dorade* or *Stormy Weather*—beautiful in their wood and brass with canvas sails. I've never doubted that these beauties-in-motion inspired my love and first profession of theatre decor, which is design and motion combined.

But we didn't socialize, party, or drink. We belonged to one of the Manhasset Bay yacht clubs, one of the few recognized sailing clubs that had Jewish members. When we sailed down east to Maine, stopping at the lively harbors like Newport or Marblehead, we kept to our family group with little regard for the local clubs' social activities. I had no inkling of that life. In 1948, cruising on the yawl we bought after *Sunbeam*, fleets of dinghies would approach us in harbor as if we were whalers in the South Seas, and tipsy yachtsmen would call out, "Hi, Bill, here to tie on a good one?" all in the tradition of her former owner. We hardly knew what to make of it, as we were never part of that world.

In theory, of course, reciprocal courtesies entitled yacht club members to limited use of other clubhouses and launch services. It wasn't until just after the war, when I was fifteen, that I realized that our club flag was like a yellow armband. The schooner was returned to us in 1945. We had moved to Connecticut, and my father applied to a yacht club in Stamford and was turned down. Attitudes had started to change during the war when clubs were forced to enlarge their onshore activities and memberships, but the news hadn't reached southwestern Connecticut. There was a small club in Norwalk where we moored, off Bell Island, and I got the drift of all this when the club launchman, a huge and oddly fang-toothed man, just happened to nudge me off the club's narrow dock after I landed our dinghy there one day to ask a favor.

It could have been an accident, and falling in never surprises me, but he called out, "No Jews here," as I swam to the dinghy, which he had untied and pushed out. News had traveled from Stamford to Norwalk. I never told Dad or my brother.

Only a few weeks later we lost an anchor, and this man, without any word from us, dragged for it and found it—a rare kindness. At the end of the season I approached him (staying at my oars, at a distance) and asked if we could come to his dock to buy fuel. "Call the commodore," he said, and gave me the name. I phoned him at the bank and asked if fuel could be bought. "Of course, that's what it's for, for purchase." I said I'd like him to phone the dock with specific permission. "Sure, what's your boat's name?"

I told him. A long, long pause, and then, "Well, I said yes, so it's yes," and he hung up, and we took on our fuel. There have been changes since, some superficial, some better than superficial. To dwell on the past is stupid, but to forget it is monstrous.

Perhaps our social shyness kept us from the bo-ho camaraderie of racing. We did race a few times in the yawl we bought after *Sunbeam*, and somewhere there's a pewter dish to remind us of a win. But my lifelong fascination with the water itself doesn't welcome the extra step of using it as a playing field for competition. Today, from our island home, we sometimes watch fleets of sailboats scurry out under power to some starting line and then churn in at evening under bare spars. This is not for us. In our engineless vessel the strategies we use with our river-mouth currents and our thoughtful alliance with the gentler morning and evening breezes are satisfaction and achievement enough.

Maybe this seems elitist in its own way—the fascination of what's difficult and all of that—but I learned more about sailing from handling our old thirty-eight-foot cutter *Rose of York* after I threw her engine overboard than from all the ocean crossings I'd made. Sailing her into finger piers and occasionally having to sail her backwards taught me a lot. Here's a moral tale: every year we made the round trip to a winter berth in Virginia. We often sailed through Hell Gate and the East River. "I'll only switch on the engine in an emergency," I vowed, and there always seemed to be one in these tricky guts and narrows, and we always turned it on. But for the six remaining passages after we lost the engine, she breezed through with grace. Well, grace and anxiety both, but we made it.

Leonora left with her excitement and love and naïve faith in us, and we helped pack her gifts in a new suitcase. This was a hinge of the trip for me, that last kiss and hug. I thought of our deception. Was it so bad? How could we tell her that Cape Horn, the known symbol of ferocious ocean, was an easier passage for a small engineless boat than the dreadful Strait of Magellan? The open ocean is your friend. Rock shores are your enemy. From the sailing directions for the Straits: "Sudden darkness . . . winds may reverse 180° in seconds . . . sudden gusts of hurricane force . . . anchors will lie on kelp . . . dangerous currents and eddies . . ." We noted, however, that there was no mention of plague.

While Dan was off for two days (har, har, as he would say), I sat on *Sparrow* feeling sorry for myself, queasy in the plunge of the open harbor. One day I sewed for fourteen hours to make a canvas envelope to hold our life ring. This would speed throwing it out if one of us slipped off. After Dan returned, we were soon deep in our own thoughts—but comfortable together.

The next day we shopped and phoned Julia and Jack, and the next morning we set out. Pidel, a man that Dan described as "an ancient," was not really that old, just seaburned and sunburned. He had taken our laundry, telling Dan it would be $15, which was only a bit more than the Connecticut price for washing two sleeping bags and a few shirts and jeans and towels. Now he said Dan had misunderstood him—he meant $50. A tour director interpreted. I finally said that we must settle the honorable way and split the difference, which I allowed to be half of the $35 difference, added to the $15. This was explained and Pidel was intrigued by "the honorable way," and accepted and bowed. So I said it was $15 plus $17.50, or $32.50.

"Make it $35," he said.

DAN

DAY 150. Dad and I say goodbye to Mom and put her on the plane back to New York. Even though the Falklands are our next stop and Cape Horn is along the way, I'm not worried about not seeing her again—except for my distrust of airplanes. I feel safer on *Sparrow* where I know everything works and I'm the one accountable. We wonder if her luggage will ever catch up to her.

In the evening we pick up a Texas radio station that plays 60 percent commercials. We don't want anything. Then an awful dinner on board: "Come on, Dad, I ate *my* half."

DAY 151. Dad and I rent a pair of shaggy steeds and they're so messy that from ten feet, I can't tell if they have their saddles on or not. Anyway, Dad's never been on a horse before and spends most of the day going, "Come on, please go . . . Giddy-up horse . . . OK?" Whereupon I sneak up behind him and whack the horse, sending it into a hair-raising walk, and Dad's proud the horse has understood his request.

We ride along the cliffs east of town following a narrow footpath. I push a rock over the edge and watch it shrink until it splashes in the ocean. We cut inland and find a place where the ground has collapsed into what was once an air bubble trapped in lava. It is like a sunken courtyard. Part of the bubble goes deep into the ground and I follow it until all I can see behind me is a thin beam of light with a worried Dad silhouetted in it.

DAY 152. Our years of planning are complete. There is nothing more to do and not having an activity that focuses our minds and diffuses our fears is brutal. We are going into a place we do not know.

DAY 153. Up at 0500 for a final energetic cleaning. Dad finds the source of an amazing odor under my bunk. It's a sort of cheese created from several cans of condensed milk that rusted through. Perhaps "fruit yogurt" best describes it, since a can of pineapple was also involved.

There are no more adjustments to make or equipment to buy to make us feel prepared. The time has come. We are ready for The Horn. My mind is so on-line with the boat that I can now envision everything on board *Sparrow* from the comfort of the bunk.

Starting in the fo'c'sle: extra foam rubber for cushions; a sea anchor; five empty water jugs; a big magnet; spare lumber, teak and oak; three hundred feet of anchor line; our larger sails: the genoa, the ghoster, #1 and #2 jibs, the spinnaker, and the spare mainsail; three anchors (ninety-five pounds total); toilet paper and paper towels; small buoys; twelve cans of motor oil for heavy seas; eleven gallons of kerosene; Navik parts; precut wood for emergency hatches; precut plexiglass for portholes; a bosun's chair (for going up the mast if necessary); hoses; spare handles for the Edson pump, whale pump, and anchor windlass, spare parts for all three; two extra pouring spouts for water or kerosene jugs; five hundred feet of assorted line; four hammocks (holding most of the above); two six-foot oars; an assortment of canned food; eighty-six eggs; twelve grapefruits; thirty-four oranges; teak oil; acetone; stove alcohol; the Walker log; chunks of neoprene (emergency gaskets); spare solid and clear inspection plates; Y-valves, T-valves, straight valves, elbows, and end fittings; through-hull fittings; hole plugs; hose valves; plastic tank-filler caps; sections of hose for joints; brass valves; a marlinespike and a knife to cut the anchor line in an emergency.

Now, stepping aft two feet into the "vestibule," which has shelves and bins on both sides, you'll find the spitfire jib, two storm jibs, and the storm trysail; sheets of leather, sailcloth, and dodger material; chunks of thick rawhide; a complete sewing kit with thread, needles, twines, grommets, hooks, eyes, and fids; two mast hoops; assorted bags; one gallon of Jean Naté Friction pour le Bain (a gift from Glenn); more spare canvas; stationery; towels, sheets, and pillowcases; washcloths; dish towels; a bag containing extra cleats, blocks, more winch parts; another bag *full* of shackles, turnbuckle parts, cables, sailslides, hooks, snap shackles, and assorted emergency gear; a third bag with everything else from inchworms to cabinet fittings, eye bolts to key-ring clips, a spare watchband to a collection of so many odds 'n' ends—it's the "everything else" bag; two tackle boxes full of bronze and stainless steel bolts and screws, flathead, pan, oval, round, and hex; teflon washers; propane bottles; the three-gallon kerosene tank for the heat stove, and two bicycle pumps to pressurize it; a box of cotton caulking; eighty feet of quarter-inch stainless steel cable; the big navigation books (tables, sailing passages, etc.); powdered miso soup; dry milk; molasses; spices; lots more food; more navigation books; bug repellant; vitamins; cotton pads; toothpaste; razors and shaving cream; more vitamins plus baby powder, petroleum jelly, nose spray, Kaopectate, seasick medicine, Lomotil, more seasick medicine, tetracycline, anti-amoeba stuff, malaria pills, penicillin, four anaphylactic kits, a dental emergency kit (Dad won't let me near him with it), mouthwash, cough medicine, and a complete "medicine chest" box that has everything for anything, and Tylenol; extra lamp chimneys; a suction-grip vise; neoprene; spare scuba-mask straps; a file cabinet of all the manuals and guarantees for everything on board; rice and beans; one hundred AA batteries; ten six-volt "hotshots"; fifty D batteries; seventy-five C batteries; another mast hoop; New Year's Eve presents from Mom; twenty different-sized corks; gauze; every kind of first-aid cream and cleanser; four suture kits; tweezers and nail cutters; another emergency first-aid kit; hot packs and cold packs; a hot-water bottle; a spare-parts kit with bulbs for the compass, all flashlights, cockpit lights, running lights, voltmeter, and masthead pennant; diaphragms, switches, burners, wicks, asbestos; more anchor windlass parts; a copper-tubing kit; and extra latches for all hatches; under the floorboard, three hundred feet of anchor chain.

Then we step into the main cabin (fifteen feet to go): two sleeping bags; four radios; two hundred books; seventy-five cassettes; navigation tools (plastic triangles, dividers, etc.); two wallets; matchboxes; eight lighters; two mirrors; colored gels for makeshift running lights; an electric razor; flints; a pencil sharpener; hundreds of cans, boxes, jars, and bags of food; fiberglass repair material (fume masks,

resin, acetone, hardener, matting, and roving cloth); my
clothes; Dad's clothes; knives (double-edge boot knife, a
stiletto from the Galápagos, ship's knife, cooking knives);
paper clips, pens, pencils, pads of paper, white-out, two
decks of cards; rubber bands, red ribbon, more stationery;
half a mile of duct tape, electrician's tape, Scotch tape,
masking tape, chaffing and spinnaker tape; marlin twine; a
strobe light; emergency life raft signal dye; candles; shoe
polish; a gallon of salt-water shampoo; two fire extin-
guishers; five timepieces; a barometer and barograph; the
heat stove; photos; a light sewing kit; the radio direction
finder; two spare compasses; cabin lights; three kerosene
lamps; radio/electronics accessories; air deodorant; cat
medicine; flea collars; two mousetraps (one and a spare); a
checkbook; padlock; lens paper; the tape-deck head
cleaner; three flashlights; one searchlight; ten one-hundred-
dollar bills; hats; soap; three sets of foul-weather gear;
gloves; two more quarts of preheat stove alcohol; rubber
and bristle brushes; a compartment full of paints, varnishes,
glues, caulking mixes, and bedding compounds; spices,
jams, salt, pepper, onions, garlic, ginger, potatoes, *tons more*
food; pots, pans, forks, spoons, chopsticks, spatulas, etc;
dishes, cups, bowls, plates, a five-gallon kerosene tank and
pump; two big twelve-volt batteries; fuse box; main switch;
boots; soda; anti-flea powder (for us); funnels; two fishing
poles; a replacement for *every foot* of hose on board; an electric wire-solder gun; most drill bits made; plastic bags (five
sizes); two sextants; cat food, cat litter; flares; Emergency
Position Indicator Radio Beacon; an emergency freshwater
still; tackle box; fishing lures; spears; sail covers; a third
sleeping bag; a library of charts ten inches thick; flux and
solder; clips and clamps; screwdrivers, vise grips, hammers,
nails, mallets, chisels, saws, putty knives, wrenches of all
sizes and sorts, calipers, cotter pins, rings, clips, pegs, plugs,
hose clamps, nail sets, and screw sets; a set of international
signal flags (alphabet); eighteen national flags; two Avon
repair kits; foul-weather repair kits; two old condoms; one

alto recorder, one soprano recorder, a flute; two Christmas stockings; two pillows, three deck cushions, and one home-made comfort pillow sewed into a canvas shopping bag (for the cockpit); winch handles; a garlic press; a third sewing kit; three pipes and an ashtray; birthday presents; clothes ham-mock; toothbrushes; combs; six hundred feet of light line on a spool; beeswax; cat pan, bowls for the cat; two cameras, sixty rolls of film; rags; marlinespike and another knife handy to the cockpit; an aviation chart light that works below or in the cockpit; a hammock for fruit.

In the lazarette (the big aft locker you reach through a hatch in the cockpit) you'll find docking lines, fenders, a fender board; H_2O shower bags; water jugs; life jackets; the nine-foot Avon rubber raft, its air pump, and com-pressed air cylinders for it; two scuba masks; two snorkles and two sets of fins; one wet suit and pair of booties; the scuba bag; a fish bag; the emergency automatic blow-up life raft; one canvas and one plastic bucket.

In a little locker under the tiller: our lead line; sail ties; scrubbers; a suction-cup device that helps you grip the hull while you swim and scrub; spare small lines.

In the cockpit: the winch handles; the big Edson pump handle; a plastic canteen by the compass; a pad and pencil held in place with shock cord; a scoop for bailing out the extra two inches of water that won't drain from the cockpit; a sponge. Forward, taped to the mast, is another sheath knife and marlinespike. Lashings and bits of line are tied to various places on deck, ready to use.

It is amazing just how *secure* everything is. Imagine living in a one-room apartment with all this stuff—kitchen next to bedroom next to dining room next to bathroom next to library. Turn it over 180°, shake, and what would happen? On *Sparrow*, not much. A pencil might fall, and certainly the cat, but that's all.

We're ready.

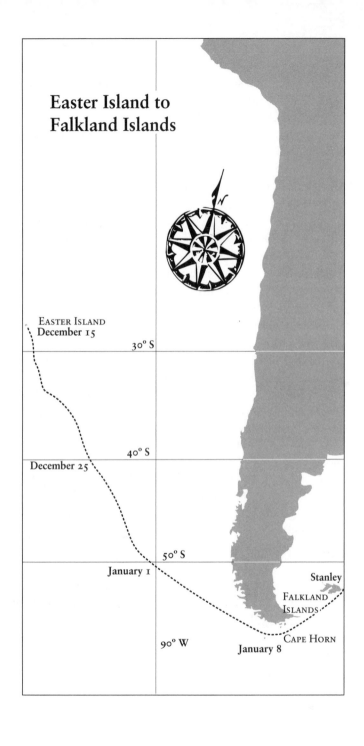

Easter Island to
Falkland Islands

EASTER ISLAND
December 15

30° S

40° S

December 25

50° S

January 1

Stanley

FALKLAND
ISLANDS

90° W

CAPE HORN
January 8

9 TO THE HORN

If you would know the age of the earth, look
upon the face of the sea in a storm.
  —*Joseph Conrad,* The Mirror of the Sea

DAN

DAY 153. We are off in light winds. Tiger has grown the hair back on his nose. We don't know why it balded, but he looked like a baboon. Now it's thick, but still short. A crew-cut nose. Dad gives me a haircut and I ask for it shorter and shorter and now it's only a fuzz. He's upset and says I look like Haldeman.

DAY 154. We see our first albatross today, bobbing in the water. Our bird book calls it a wandering albatross, and it has a wingspan of ten feet. That's two feet more than *Sparrow*'s width. It flew in, landed near us, and watched us with cold yellow eyes as we sailed slowly by.

DAY 156. Tonight's the first night of Chanukah. The ocean is calm—too calm really. We're sort of drifting. Dad yells at the sails, then takes them down. Things clank and we roll. The menorah slides back and forth on the cabin table. We tape it down. We light two candles tonight. The cat walks across and briefly catches fire.

"Dad, do you think my descendants will someday tape the menorah, light the cat, and consider it an ancient ritual, origin lost in history?"

Gifts! Candy. A book of horror stories. Cookies. There will be gifts every night for eight nights. The last night is Christmas, and there are gifts for that too. Julia and Jack have wrapped and labeled each gift. The days are getting longer and soon there'll be only four hours of night and that will be only a sort of protracted dusk-dawn. Our afternoon task is waterproofing mittens. I bought a compound that you squeeze into the seams.

I have no companions to be drunk with and talk to about girls. It's 5:00 A.M. and dads just don't work for every sort of conversation, you know. Fiery red sunrise and no wind, sails swilling about and the cat on his morning space-cadet romp—leaping at nothings and chewing ghosts. Today I pulled out the chart of Port Stanley in the Falklands. We'll be going there once we get around The Horn. It has a beautiful bottleneck harbor, which means it must be a safe anchorage indeed. However, the "sailing directions" caution the tourist about "many thousands of unexploded land mines in the vicinity." They also say that the holding ground (that's the harbor bottom) is so good that boats are often unable to retrieve their anchors.

DAY 158. It's pouring rain. We hide below, checking the steering every half-hour or so. We sail 121 miles today.

DAY 159. The barometer has fallen from 1026 to 1012 in twenty-four hours. That's bad. The sky is not normal, and the waves are bigger than they should be in this wind. I am eager and afraid. I've never been in what's called a "Roaring Forties" gale. *Sparrow* is jumping along. Dad is asleep below, and I just put on the #2 red jib. I thought of putting up the #1, which is bigger, but am glad I didn't because we are almost rail under. The wind gusts Force 6 and I may soon take in a reef.

Once upon a time sailors could not look at the digital LED readouts in their cockpits or go below to check the wind speed from a dial. Imagine! They relied on what they saw and the pitch of the windsong through the rigging or their hair. So they invented the *Beaufort scale* for clarity. It's not much different than the way Dad and I talk about the weather.

"What's it like out?"

"Windy."

"Extremely windy?"

"Very fucking windy."

The Beaufort scale goes from 0 to 12, with 0 being a calm, smooth, mirror-like sea. These twelve conditions are referred to as "Forces," and a Force 12 is a hurricane. The descriptions are visual, not digital. Force 4 is a "moderate breeze, small waves, becoming longer; fairly frequent white horses." At Force 5, a "fresh breeze," we are told that a "fishing smack . . . shortens sail." (Dad always says that a Force 6 is just a Force 5 blowing against the way you want to go.) Around Force 8 you begin to feel anxious, and "foam is blown in well-defined streaks with the wind." I've never been at sea in anything near Force 10, the official description of which calls for twenty-nine-foot waves where "the tumbling of the sea becomes heavy and shock-like . . . the whole surface of the sea takes a white appearance." In other words, "extremely fucking windy," which sounds like "ydniw gnikcuf ylemertxe" as the words are blown back down your throat.

DAY 160. Even floating in this remote part of the earth cut off from input except the news, I am happy to say that "The Larry King Show," whatever that is, thoroughly bores me and I cannot endure it for more than five minutes. I prefer the squeaking of the self-steerer—I could oil it and then there would only be the ripples of the water along the hull and creaking rigging, but I like the squeak. Sure beats Larry.

DAY 161. Half the stars fade into haze, which fades into the gray sea, which is illuminated by coin-shaped reflections trailing in the wake. The wind comes in gentle puffs causing the ghoster to flap, sending vibrations through the mast and then on through the whole boat to the water for any sea creature to feel. I sit crouched in a glow of soft red light from the compass, huddled under a canvas hood, which protects me from the cool gusts of wind. Sometimes they reach me and send chills down my spine. Gently *Sparrow* rocks from side to side, interrupted by soft lurches forward. I am surrounded by time and feel it stretching in all directions.

DAY 163. It's Christmas morning now and I can tell I've matured since I was four because I'm letting Dad sleep late, even though I can see the bag of presents stowed forward with the sails. Christmas officially began at midnight when Dad woke me up with burnt popcorn. I have a squirt gun for him. But there isn't really a Christmas spirit. We can stick cloves in an orange and make eggnog, but there are no cars stuck in the snow. We've been at sea ten days and we may have twenty to go. Soon, we'll be in the Roaring Forties (latitudes 40° to 50° south). If you look at a globe you'll see there are no *continents* around the whole world here. The waves tend to get humongous with no beaches to eat them up.

I am eager to get past Cape Horn. It's gotten in the way of thinking of the future, because it seems to me that The Horn's comment on the whole question of my future is, "Maybe not." Dad says I'm going to brag about our passage to everyone; I accuse him of planning to be more sly about it, saving it for casual mentions that produce more effect. I think his ego is larger, but on second thought cannot imagine how it could be. I'm going to accidentally wake him soon, so we can open presents. Should I spill coffee or drop Tiger on him? Things always fall on him anyway, so he won't be suspicious. Books escape from the shelf and hit him, his pants fall off the rack and land on his supper, and once the jam cabinet over his head opened and a pepper shaker hit him on the ear.

DAY 164. *Lust.* On the eighth night of Chanukah I got a *Sports Illustrated Bathing Suit Calendar,* which is just one notch below *Playboy.* I looked at each picture twice, then one by one peeled them off and threw them into the sea around latitude 39° 49' south, longitude 99° 50' west. Truly I would be a great monk, creating situations over which to suffer and thereby create meaning. (I can't believe I didn't save one page!)

We've been out eleven days now and haven't been in any awful weather. I want to see some *seas!* Yesterday it rained and I took a shower. It was light rain and the wind was cold and I shivered, clinging to the mast, catching each drop that slid down the sail and along the boom toward me. With almost no hair on my head, that part is easy, but as soon as my crotch and armpits got soapy the rain stopped, and I had to wait, trembling, for another spray of precious fresh water. I was cold and very alive, my skin tight and strong. I cuddled into my still-clean sleeping bag (I've been sleeping on top with a blanket) and was ecstatic. My pruned feet dried in their own heat. Then clean clothes and, damn I feel good. My life is ruled by clean clothes—I will be happy for two days and then, as my clothes get clammy again, that will fade.

Dear Mom,

Christmas was awful. A big wave disrupted the crèche I'd set up in the fo'c'sle, causing a twelve-foot plaster giraffe to knock over the Virgin and two kings. Dad says the crèche isn't very Jewish, so I shouldn't tell you. Now it's midnight and I'm having my own mass—of course, using the menorah to hold the altar candles. When I get home I may change my name to Winslow III. All we did today was eat sugar: an entire box of cookies, the contents of the socks (ninety-two jelly beans, two chocolate soldiers, and twenty-two sesame-honey things), all eaten. The sugar shock was intense, and we drifted for hours unable to tend the ship. Love, Dan

DAVID

The literary news from down under was that at last, after ten or twelve starts that always held me past the "sleep section" but no farther, I finally hooked into *Swann's Way* and was rapturously involved. I knew that someday I'd make it. To amuse ourselves we invented holidays. The first was National Clamp Week. Then it became Rotten Fruit Week.

Of course there were real holidays too. One of the more precious gifts that came with Leonora was a cassette from our dear friends the Bicks and Lorin families. Besides a medley of favorite songs and recorded messages from other friends, there was a long segment of navigation advice by these fellow sailors. The problem was that their atlas had no proper scale, so they could only advise us that the Strait of Magellan was about three and one-half inches down and to the right of Easter Island. Worse, Easter Island's name was on their map but no outline or dot indicated a land mass. Since our cassette player could record, we started a tape to reply to them. Dan began with a report on

Easter Island and stated the bad news that indeed there was no land mass, but we were leaving it anyway and you could just see, over the horizon, the tops of the letters *E* and *ST*. Then he described the crèche of full-sized saints and animals, carved in native lava, that we had bought there. The giraffe's neck had already broken, but we were stringing Christmas lights around it. Later, he said, we were pursued by natives in canoes who bartered for the crèche; we sold it just before Christmas, not wanting it to be remaindered. We were happy with the sale because they traded us multicolored beads, lengths of copper wire, and many small mirrors. Anyway, the front, or pointed, end of the boat, where we kept the crèche, had been tipped down about thirty degrees because of the extra weight and therefore we had not been sailing our fastest.

Our tape is full of sea noises—mostly a dull roar, because the sea is noisy. But in our spoof you hear a mad character, Dan, clumping about on deck on his leg. The thump is not too loud because he found a rubber tip for the ivory leg in an old Sperry Top-Sider catalog. He's got a spare, of course. We do a wild New Year's Eve party with hundreds of guests clinking their glasses and blowing horns, but the next morning we report sadly that upon arising and being seated for brunch, a glance toward the back, past the porch and veranda area outside, shows that our most backwards two masts, plus the afterguard and the ship's band, have been swept into the sea. That takes the heart out of our holiday decorating, but we continue—art for art's sake.

The cat was everywhere, and at once. Like the cursor on a computer screen, he showed us where to work. When it was time to reef the mainsail and change jibs, at change of watch, we were *all* on deck—Tiger snug in the dodger, curled around the main halyard winch. "Scat." While Dan was working on that sail I turned to prepare the jib halyard. Tiger had settled into the coils of line. "Off!" Back to the main halyard. "Away!" Then the jib again. "Avast, dammit!" Now to ease the sheet. But why bother to locate the cleat? Just look for the cat. When we went forward while clipped to our lifelines, Tiger was always on the narrow deck, and had to be dribbled forward in soccer style. Coming aft, we'd do arabesques to clear the tether from between our legs, the little ballet ending, with a squeal, on guess who?

So we were crowded with cat. And so was the compass. When a boat is below the equator the compass card, which rotates on a needle-sharp pivot in a glass globe full of fluid, is pulled down and rubs against its bed as the magnet points down *through the earth* toward north. We phoned the manufacturer, Danforth, from Easter Island, and they were surprised that we didn't know all about that, though their literature doesn't mention it, nor do the standard texts I've read over the years. The knowledge just wasn't in our DNA, I suggested. The man, who was kind and patient, explained that our compass was balanced for, well, Connecticut and nearby. We'd have to take it apart and re-place the little weights that balance the card. We had two other compasses, but this was the main steering compass, carefully adjusted. Dan set to work on a towel on our tiny table, in the rolly anchorage at Hanga Roa. I played surgical nurse. The trick was to keep all the fluid so that when we reassembled the bowl there wouldn't be an annoying bubble on top. If we lost fluid, we could temporarily supplement it with gin or kerosene, first checking for clotting. But I've seen a compass treated that way by Hum Barton, and the gin ate off the compass paint, and so it snowed like one of those snow-globe souvenirs, a blizzard above a blank card. I believe that there is no word in our language for those Statue of Liberty–type snow globes. The operation succeeded. A sawed-in-half brass washer was glued on to re-weight the delicately suspended card. Hardly a drop of fluid was lost, and after a day of burping the instrument, there was not even the tiniest bubble in the globe. But—

and here's what I'm coming at—there was a cat hair in the compass bowl. Long may it float.

DAN

DAY 166. We are now in the Roaring Forties. They haven't even hummed yet, but I can feel a certain shiftiness about us like they don't care how much sleep I get. I am still in bare feet though my toes are numb. It would be admitting it's cold if I put on boots. Sailing in "shorts weather" is so easy compared to cold and rain. I always hope the night will be gentle and that I can watch it from the safety of the cockpit. But it is exhilarating to go forward in darkness and know exactly where everything is and how it should be.

I'm scared that when I return all my friends will say, "Dan, Dan who?" It's 0330 and I'm snuggled tight trying to be a ball and save heat. The purpose is to keep the heart beating in the body, on the boat, in the ocean. I like it when things are so miserable that I see that. It is more vital to be concerned about what to do not to die than what to do to "have the best time."

We are trying out a voyaging trick—our cabin floor is a knee-high sea of wadded-up newspaper. It keeps the floor and our feet dry, and when wads get soggy where we come down from deck, we just throw out a few and replace them. It's a snowy landscape and not as ugly as it sounds. Tiger loves it. He burrows and we see wads rippling to trace his course like a mole in a garden. Or he suddenly leaps into sight from nowhere and this is startling. Most of the time he just whacks at the wads from the berths. His head sticks out above the wad level when he squats on his litter pan, and he look silly-dignified as if he were in a bubble bath.

DAY 167. First gale—zooming along at six knots under just the storm jib and triple-reefed main. During gusts we take water on the foredeck. It's cool—fifty-five degrees—and clear. The Milky Way is overhead, full of its light dust; all around are pockets of dark clouds reaching down to the water. The stars go *right* down to the horizon where, "snap," they go out, over the edge. You usually don't see that, except perhaps in a desert. Clouds are skittering along quickly—the wind is Force 7 and 8 in gusts. I am eager for dawn, to view the increasing seas. I feel safe and secure tethered to *Sparrow* and in my foul-weather gear.

DAY 169

Dear Mom,

Dad's forgetful. If something is missing, it's under the cat. If something is lost, Dad had it last. He finds his glasses on his head and his socks on his feet but otherwise he doesn't find things at all. I wear a name tag now, "Hello, my name is Daniel," and there's a big sign saying BATHROOM to help him out. The seas got big today and are foam-curled. About every two hours, chance will have it that one breaks on board—a loud crash followed by roaring as the water finds its way off. These waves usually catch one of us who will have peered out at just that particular moment. Dad calls this "Wave-Sailor Syndrome." Sometimes we'll hear the crash, then there will be an orange streak of Tiger shooting below, like a billiard ball. He bounces off two or three surfaces, disappearing in a side locker to emerge cautiously looking like a plucked chicken . . . Love, Dan

I will describe peeing: first, you're below and it's wet on deck, so you decide to use the toilet, but keep waiting because you've drunk too much coffee and peed just six minutes ago. Finally, you can't wait any longer: you get up, then fall on the sleeping off-watch crew (Dad). You quickly get off and say, "Bad cat!" You stagger forward, accidentally lunging for the towel shelf and pulling all the towels and washcloths to the floor. Fix towel shelf. Say, "Bad cat!" to cover the noise. Now you gotta pee real bad. Brace yourself over the toilet, yank down your foul-weather-gear pants, which pin your legs together so you can't balance, then pick up lid and start peeing. The boat lunges and you fall backward, leaving a stripe of pee (which because of the motion hangs in the air a moment longer than is comprehensible) from the toilet up to the hatch, about three feet, over wall and woodwork. Of course, since you're falling, you can't work your "stop peeing" muscle, so you squeeze the end of your thingy and keep the pee in by sheer pinching pressure. You straighten up and tighten that muscle, which of course builds up just a tad too much pressure as you fall forward, so a thin squirt escapes at an odd angle—you try aiming for the bowl, but the lid just slammed shut, nearly biting off your thing, so you pee on the lid, and maybe put your hand in it to stop yourself from hitting your head on the cabin top (which you do anyway). Of course, which hand did you use? Exactly, so the rest of what's been waiting (between the pinched muscle and the pinched fingertips) dribbles down your leg onto the cat who is, as always, underneath you. Repeat steps 2–6. Dad says I'm so macho that I'll think he's a pervert if he suggests that I could simply sit on the toilet.

It's cold now—we're as far south as the bottom third of Canada is north and to sit on deck you need shirts, a sweater, jacket, foul-weather gear, and gloves because the air is very wet. Big waves seem to acknowledge just how isolated we are. Sixteen days and not a boat, jet trail, or any other sign of *civilization*.

Soon we have to keep an eye out for icebergs. I want to see one, penguin-covered. Seabirds have been with us constantly now, albatross and petrels—it's hard to imagine what a bird is doing a thousand miles out. Could the fishing be better out here? Anyway, they are good company, soaring in long swoops with wings an inch over the waves. Tiger sleeps on my head and I awake as he stretches and claws rows on my scalp. We go "jogging" each morning as the sun rises—we growl at each other and the winner is whoever runs fastest around the "jogging track" to bite the other. At night I write love letters to old, probably married-by-now girlfriends. Being a tragic romantic is great, but it's done alone and I have to remind people about me so they'll worry.

DAY 171. Dad wakes long enough to pee in the rubber hot-water bottle and then he puts it down by his feet to keep his toes warm. He learned this when he studied in England. "Very British," he says, then continues snoring.

DAY 174. Near gale, I write from inside my shell of plastic, which keeps the heat in. Rain and spray all over. The wind noise is intense, but I find some peace in writing. My hands are lost in big red-and-blue mittens, my body in yellow nylon, and my feet in black rubber. Looking out, my sight is framed by a plastic hood.

Dear Kim,

Hi again. It's galing outside and feels especially lonely. It's January 5 and we are about 450 miles from Cape Horn with about 1,000 miles to go before the Falklands. The wind blows the foam off the top of the waves in white streaks. Visibility is only a few feet 'cause of the spray—waves are long and there is a roaring in the rigging. My foul-weather gear leaks, but it keeps the wind out. It's a long watch and I'm tired, wet. I feel like flat soda poured on laundry . . . It's neat looking at the charts and seeing how close we are to The Horn. Finally, we're done with the chart that shows *all* of South America and onto one that is more detailed, more local. Tomorrow, we might even get onto Chart No. 32022 where there are 10 miles to an inch instead of 60. It indicates strong currents—at one point, up to eight knots (9 mph, a lot)—and the chart actually shows *℩℩*, which means *tide rip*, but at eight knots, I call it a *tide roar*. Can you imagine a chart with waves drawn permanently on it? First one I've seen. *Sparrow* has a small flock of birds in tow . . .

I've been very morbid, death thinking, and am so angry at Dad who's getting old, and I can't accept it and love him. Instead, I give him shit . . . He can give it back, and sometimes that makes me feel better.

"Dad, which comes first, November or October?"

(pause)

"Well, Dan, you'll just have to start with January. Work it out, dimwit."

"Just testing, Dad."

It's getting worse out, the barometer is falling and it's raining. Seas are big and scary. The cat is oblivious, cleaning himself on my chest. He's an excellent cat. Dad quotes his father's formula for wave height: observed height divided by two equals exact height. Love, Dan

DAY 175. Dawn, three hundred miles west of Cape Horn. Full moon and angry oceans. When you think of these waves, imagine a big, green Mack truck skidding at you sideways, with fifty bathtub loads of shaving cream on top. *Sparrow* bobs right over them. Last night, in a three-hour Force 8, a big wave whomped us, filling the cockpit and finding leaks not yet tested. We've screwed boards over the portholes and have all sorts of lids, caps, and cloths lashed-to, stuffed-in, and wadded-around vents, chimneys, and deck fittings.

Icebergs! Hitting an iceberg in a gale is what I fear. One reason Cape Horn is so feared is that the gales are usually westerly. If you want to go west, against them, you must fight for every mile. Captain Bligh spent thirty-one days in a gale, going just eighty-five miles, said, "Forget this!"

turned tail (probably seasick and depressed), and went *all the way around the world* to get to Tahiti. At least we're going east. The gales are with us. Right now the roaring in the rigging is like the soundtrack from a bad dream. Even if you're moving well, it's unsettling. I imagine falling over and freezing. The water temperature is fifty degrees or less, so quickly numbing. You cannot sail to windward in a real blow—right angles to the wind is about the best you can do. I discovered this trying to recover a sail bag. Dad was changing jibs, and before he could smother the empty bag and stuff it below, it filled with wind with a bang like a pistol shot and almost yanked off his arm.

A troop of porpoises—around twenty-five—races with us. From the top of the waves, they leap eight feet in the air. I can see them in the water in the wave crests above us, silhouetted against the sky. They're called Chilean dolphins and are not supposed to be this far offshore.

Sleeping is hard, everything rattles and things fall on you (cats, books, clothes, Dads, pens, toys, flashlights, chopsticks, bowls, crackers—or everything from the spice rack, which escapes together and for no known reason). Exhaustion finally does it, but by then it's time to get up. Dad keeps clothes in the jam cupboard over his head so the jars won't rattle. The weather here is fast to change. I begin my watch at midnight, all bundles with my big furry hat almost covering my eyes, wearing thick mittens and baggy pants. Now it's short sleeves and bright at 0600. Although the temperature range here is like a northern Canadian summer, in the fifties and sixties, the wind is so strong that fifty degrees can feel freezing cold.

DAVID

Sometimes I felt like a marionette badly operated. Around my neck was a loop of string that was pinned to my hat to keep it from blowing away. Another loop kept my reading glasses in place. To keep myself on board I wore a tether harness—a buckle-and-strap affair like a parachute harness—with a metal ring in the middle of my chest. The tether is a strap that attaches to this ring, about eight feet long, with a snap at the end that I could hook on to anything. All the straps and strings snagged on everything. The main difference in my mobility on this voyage compared to my others was my damned glasses. After eight years I still couldn't get used to them and they steamed up or fell off, particularly when I was working on something upside down, which one often does on a boat.

I was never sure if Dan used the tether when he went forward at night. He said he did, but I didn't always hear the metal snap dragging along the deck as he pulled it behind him, clipped to a line that ran along the deck from stern to bow. I would try to avoid imagining coming on deck in the morning to find it empty. What would have happened to him is not the worst of ends, and I've envisioned myself there too, just staying afloat as long as possible, perhaps seeing the boat try to return, but too far off. But if I were on deck, searching the waters for him, those few last hours of my own life are unimaginable. And if I were in the water, seeing the boat at a distance, Dan frantic on the spreaders, would he be shaking uncontrollably too? We've talked about this. Whatever I do, he has promised not to follow me over if I'm lost. (The problem of a two-person voyage: only one witness.) After his dog's death, he spoke of his fear that I would die during the voyage, at sea.

"I see you there, Dad, cold, what do I do?"

"Well, Dan, you take off any clothing that's useful and my wristwatch and you roll me in and keep sailing and you know that I died doing exactly what I wanted to do and in company I love."

Damn this age business. I believe in fairy tales, and a child's need for the bloody ones too, but I wish the image of parents, like Hansel and Gretel's mother and father, wasn't always white-haired folk bent over with canes. Parents aren't like that anymore. Still, despite his annoyance at my absent-mindedness, Dan had instinctive faith in my constant presence, the knowledge that the father has always been there and will be there. He didn't wake at night in a panic that I might not be on board. For me it was the reverse. He was on this planet because of me, and I was here when he wasn't. I saw the thread broken—I imagined coming on deck and him gone.

My father had his first heart attack when he was fifty-five. My older brother had his two years before our voyage, at fifty-five. Now, at fifty-four, I didn't have the symptoms or conditions they both had. But I ran down that dock in Jamaica and jumped on *Sparrow* and yelled, "I'm safe," because at sea I always feel too alive for any of that.

I recall frightening my father when I was small. We were at a resort. I remember cabins and a lake. I became the companion of an older boy who sported the wisdom and skill of a six-year-old. There was a match-to-a-pile-of-leaves incident that won punishment for him—I was deemed incompetent and earned only a rebuke. But one day we really brought the world down on us. He jumped into a rowboat at the lake's edge, called, "Come on," and in I went. He sat at the oars and pulled manfully away from the sandy edge. I sat in the stern, and soon became aware of shouts on the fading shore. I remember clearly even now how small the people looked. I remember being unable to gather meaning from the shouts, and I waved back. I saw my father run down the beach and dive in. He had a superb physique and had been a competitive swimmer at Columbia. He swam mightily toward us, and as he gained, my captain at the oars pulled harder. Perhaps the race was only a minute, only a hundred feet, but it was miles to me, and I still remember it when I see the Australian crawl done well. Dad came churning on and was within three feet of the boat. I reached out to grasp his hand, happy that he wanted to be with us. He lunged and grabbed the transom with one hand and with the other he swung in a wide arc and slapped me so hard that I flew into the bottom of the boat. Dripping, he stepped over me, brushed aside the other boy, and rowed in. I was too stunned to cry, and lay where I had landed. I remember nothing else about this except a sharp and sudden understanding two or three years later. I was never struck again.

I thought of my father on those long dusks, as we made our southing. At the equator the sun dropped straight down, here it slid and slipped sideways into the sea, and it was never far above or below the horizon. The nights were short, and a few hundred miles south of The Horn, the sun doesn't set at all in the Antarctic summer. But there is a time, sunset, when I believe that fear grips a sailor. Not before sunup, when we are comfortable with the dark, closed in to our little circle, perhaps to the glow of one lamp turned low that keeps the damp from a tight cabin. What chills me, this moment of fear, is the time just after the sun has gone. Ashore it can be soft—"The hour of twilight, when voices bloom," Carson McCullers wrote—but here when the top edge of the friendly sun goes under the clean horizon rim, the scale suddenly shifts. The weather clouds become ominous, and the ocean is achingly vast.

My last sight of my father was near a curiously symmetrical spot on the ocean, latitude 23° 50' north, longitude 23° 50' west. I noticed the symmetry when I thumbed through my old sea journals, preparing for this voyage. It's in the North Atlantic, not far from the Canary Islands, and Columbus was near that place when he wrote that he missed the spring in Andalusia and the call of birds. Often, still, I hear my father's voice, but I saw him clearly only that one night, in the spring of 1963, seven months after he died. One of the last times I'd heard his voice, he spoke into my bad ear, and I'd told him crossly to move to the other side. He died in a Connecticut hospital late at night on the last day of September. My brother was there. We were waiting in an alcove painted dull green. The last thing Dad said to me that afternoon was that he was proud of me. He said a few other things that were not clear, but I knew what they were because he'd said them more clearly in his sleep during a week that I'd slept in the room with him at home. It was an apology for a stupid error he'd made during a sailing race that we could have won, and it touches me now because I think I understand that through this trivial means he was trying to say he was sorry for all the wrongs he may have done to his boys. Maybe he felt guilty because we worshiped him as a perfect man.

My father's doctor had gone home. The nurse came into the alcove and whispered something to my brother. He is a physician himself, and walked the way doctors do—he didn't run to the room—and I stood with Leonora outside. We heard the squeakings and plungings and gaspings but the heart didn't restart and after a long time my brother came out and embraced me. We went in and my father's mouth was gaping, open more than in sleep. He didn't look dead to me, he looked beaten, defeated. That was the shock, because in our years he'd never been defeated in all the things he did for us, in getting us all the things we wanted. His head was back on the pillow, his mouth agape, and I asked the nurse to close his mouth and we drove home to get my mother, but when she came into the room with us, it was still open. He was smaller and grayer, but all I really saw was the grotesque open mouth. I remember my mother's hands, with white skeletal knuckles clenched on the railing of the bed, and four days later on the coffin edge until I uncurled her fingers one by one. She said, "Hold on," and then she said, "I can't hold on any longer, can I?" And I said, "No, Mom, not that way."

But my father didn't begin to talk to me again until that next spring when we were lashed out to sea by a gale off Finisterre. My shipmate Marvin March and I sat below, with paperbacks in hand, but our eyes, like those of all sailors in wooden boats, were fixed on the seam between cabin and deck where the sea, hitting like hard-thrown scoops of gravel, might burst in. The wind screamed a full octave that night, and the wedges bracing the mast started to whine in the voice of Dad, speaking in his sleep. He said, only once but clearly, "Relax, boy." Dan was at home then, three years old.

A third crew member, Ed Bigelow, joined us in Vigo and soon we were westing past the Canaries. Before one midnight watch, I knew from a troubled sleep and the way a wooden ship groans that we must take in sail. When I went on deck three combers surged past our beautiful *Rose of York* and swept her forward in a foam of frightening sea white. Stars seemed below us as we flew from wavetop to wavetop. I asked Eddie to keep her steady and went forward to crank down the mainsail, which reefed by being rolled around the boom like a window shade. I braced my feet against a ventilator cowl and worked the handle that rolled the boom. *Rose* started to fly lightly, eased of the labor of carrying too much sail. We would hover a moment and then fall forward in slow motion into troughs too deep and dark to see their bottoms, troughs that brought to mind nightmares of bared rocks at the bottom of black waterless pits. You could imagine plunging down and being shattered into a million bits of wood and steel and bone. We fell and splintered the water into a thousand white birds that burst up like ducks from the water. We rose with my stomach just a notch behind and suddenly the animated face of a drowning man—no, my father's face thrown back hugely on the rounded pillow of the crest— rolling ahead and then under us into the great hollow, and we stood still and then began the great scything curve down. So animated, so alive! The gaping mouth now moving, the eye sockets emptying, trembling. *Dad!* And we fell into the gaping mouth that was tearing into the nostril, and we sliced and shattered the eye into a spray that leaped over us and raced us with the wind and fell salty into my own open mouth.

"Hold on!" It was my mother's voice.

I sprawled on the slippery cabin top. I hadn't ridden the

next lifting wave. My legs didn't work and I pulled myself with my hands into the cockpit and put a hand on the tiller. Eddie went to the rail, then said good night and went below. The numbers on the glowing compass card were jiggling and my legs began to shake. The boat shuddered and the stars swept in vibrating lines. *Rose* wallowed and heaved.

"Steady boy, take her down, you're way off course," my father said.

Such were twilight thoughts as *Sparrow* raced to The Horn. The skies were bigger, as they are in the Dutch landscapes with just a strip of land at the bottom of the painting, and that seems like an affectation until you go to Holland and see for yourself that the skies and the clouds *are* bigger. And now the earth was tipped and we slid down to the point of fury at the bottom of the world where the lines of longitude gathered like drawstrings.

Other spirits came to me in those dusks, and the sounds of the curling foam at the wave crests were like whispering—names I didn't imagine had meaning to me, or that I could even remember. Bill Schindler, a one-legged, midget auto-racing driver; Cedarhurst Stadium, 1939 and 1940. Andy Varipapa, a semiprofessional bowler: I set pins for him once in 1942 when I was twelve. I played tapes of Kathleen Ferrier, dead for over thirty years, and that sound brought together the dead and the living in those twilights. A woman once told me that she loved her body's smell because it reminded her that she came from the sea, and I thought then, out there, that we would return to these seas and not to the earth.

On New Year's Eve we blew the uncurling paper whistles that came with our gifts, and there were three party hats. We opened our fortune cookies. Mine: "You are soon to go on a long journey." Dan's: "Watch out for bad companions." Tiger's: "You will be drawn to the glamour of the stage." January 1 was pipe-maintenance day. Then I lost a filling chewing a Christmas caramel, and Dan was desperate to operate and amortize our nineteen-dollar dental emergency kit. No dice. I let him look, but the plastic dental mirror fogged as we laughed. We listened to the water, the *psoosh* of the bow wave, the *hissh* of the water streaming by, white, the *crissch* of the quarter wave starting out from alongside the cockpit, the *fwssh* of wave-tops nearby. Four sounds that you learned to hear at the same time, like an orchestra conductor—*Sparrow*'s voice.

The cat had magic dewy beads on his fur in the morning. I started a section of my daily journal recording how each spot appeared on my long johns. How could they get so dirty after only a week? There's no air dirt or dust out there. But spill by spill, spot by spot, it added up. Our best surprise meal was when we thought we'd run out of carrots and one rolled out of my berth as I sat to cut the night's vegetables. One evening I was amazed to see Dan crying at the climax of *La Traviata*, but excitement subsided as I saw that he was slicing onions. On my thirtieth wedding anniversary Dan made good biscuits in the pressure cooker. There was a card from Leonora. Good, I was on her list. "I love you, come home soon." We were not to The Horn, but I felt on the way home.

Through all of this the recording barometer was on a long and frightening dive. It inscribes on a roll of paper, and the ink line started at the top of the sheet and descended on a steady slope for ninety-six hours until it was near the bottom. This was like a background of scary anticipatory movie music that went on for days. The temperature was down to forty-three degrees at night. The beauties didn't stop; now we had flocks of exquisite delft-blue whale birds, shaped like small doves. The albatrosses were always with us. They glided, sometimes moving their wings only once every minute and a half, keeping one wing tip an inch from the waves. They must sense exactly that space to the water. The big ones had that quality that bird people call "jizz"—a wonderful word (architects would say "monumental" and performers would say "star quality"). Often, in these steep, short seas of about twelve feet, they would be soaring on the back of a wave and when *Sparrow* lifted to the crest there was a giant bird only a few feet astern, as suddenly revealed as if a magician had dropped a cloth. Dan could make them land in the water by waving his arm. He said it was because they knew man, and the arm motion meant that food was being dropped into the water.

In such waters you can't help wondering at the way following seas approach and then, suddenly and easily, are under you and gone, rolling ahead. It is remarkable how they seem to melt as you rise to them. I believe that this illusion is caused partly by our lack of a firm horizon and the ease with which we come to accept the constant roller coaster. When a boat tilts forward, as the wave starts to lift her stern—and this is the key moment to me—the eye is tilted up as one looks aft, and without the secure horizon reference, the wave is just not there as our eye skims the surface and does not see it square on. Conversely, the eye is tilted down as the stern dips when the crest is past, and so the eye perceives the following mountain of water as higher.

Dan's target was 50° south and 90° degrees west. We would turn eastward then, into the chute of Drake Passage. Our idea was to stay two hundred miles away from land as we angled in, then turn east and go across at the level of The Horn. If we wandered closer, a gale from the southwest could slam us up into the dreaded rocks that curved down the western tip of the continent. Slocum and Darwin spoke of this archipelago of great rocks, and called it the Milky Way of the sea. Now we were leaving all the world I knew—we were south of Africa, south of Australia, south of Tasmania and New Zealand. Only ocean and the one rocky tip remained.

On January 3, still building *Sparrow*, I finished a tiny piece of the bookcase—just a detail to make it pretty. It would have been impossible in heavier weather. Strangely,

I was beginning to worry that we wouldn't have any really shocking weather and wouldn't be able to crow about a Horn passage. Dan thought I was crazy and he could have been right. I told him the old joke about the rabbi who became so addicted to golf that at dawn on the morning of the holiest day of the year he was out on the links, hoping no one would see him. He teed off—a hole in one! He fell to his knees and called out, "God! How can you reward such a sinner?" The great voice spoke from the clouds. "And who are you going to tell?" When I told stories like this he'd always remind me that I'd told it before. Now he added, "Dad, you're waning philosophical."

We waited like athletes before the game. We stared at the ceiling. We may not have been in a storm but we were in the great seas, long and gray, and in the grip of the great west wind, of which Conrad said:

> The West Wind is too great a king to be a dissembler: he is no calculator plotting deep schemes in a somber heart; he is too strong for small artifices; there is passion in all his moods, even in the soft mood of his serene days . . . He is all things to all oceans; he is like a poet seated upon a throne—magnificent, simple, barbarous, pensive, generous, impulsive, changeable, unfathomable . . .

When the seas rose, the cat, sitting on the table in a sphinx position, seemed to levitate, become airborne toward my bunk cloth, and slide down into his water bowl without changing his position.

A name kept going through my head incessantly. *Edwige*. Dickens? I spent days digging in my brain. Suddenly I remembered: the costume designer's cat, summer 1954, at Green Mansion Theatre, where I met Leonora.

Under all that stress and movement, something usually needed fixing. The weathercloth, which kept the spray out of the cockpit, split. I sewed it. Every day I went forward and studied the hardware at our masthead with binoculars.

All seemed well, but we were eager to go up the mast as soon as calmer seas made it enjoyable. These were moments to take pleasure from our thoughtful preparations. But I wished Dan would stop yelling, "Where's my crossbow!" every time he saw an albatross.

The most constant sense was that of being so alone. Not a plane, a jet trail, or a piece of floating debris for twenty days. Two thousand miles out of Easter Island, we toasted. I shaved, changed long johns, employed a bit of washrag, and took a quick glance at my skin. Then it was into my last clean *Falklands-or-bust* long johns. There was a tiny toy truck prize in the hot chocolate can we had just opened, and we were delighted. It was on the table and could roll back and forth forever. Swat! It was off, thank you, Tiger. I threw a wad of paper out of the hatch and missed. The paper hit the wooden rim, but I hadn't yet let it go. My bashed fingers ached in the cold, and of course we laughed hysterically about that.

On January 6, we cut to The Horn. At 1145 we passed due south of (and half a world away from) our Manhattan home, and by noon we were south of the East 80s where our friends the Bicks and Lorin families lived. Distances in reference to north are shortened: the lines of longitude gather in, ready to meet at the pole. Soon we'd be south of Montauk Point, the tip of Long Island, and farther east than *Sparrow* had ever gone. We were coming to it. I couldn't write or read. I was stupefied by excitement.

DAN

DAY 176. Dawn—Force 6 following wind, first reef and no jib. The barometer is falling fast. Bow foam roars six feet on either side—*Sparrow*'s soft feathers. A few birds. Nervous. We should sight the little southernmost island of Diego Ramirez tonight. The clouds have left a little gap and I can see the sunrise, an awful red. "Red in the morning, sailors take warning . . ."

Now my navigation is critical, and I cannot afford the arrogance and luxury of having a thousand miles on all sides. A landsman might think a five-mile error big, but actually that's not bad—it's usually good enough for a landfall. Yet after twenty-two days of vast ocean I wonder if I've made some tiny error compounded twenty-two times. Then who knows where we'd fetch up? I'm hoping for a couple of good days now—I want to see Horn Island and throw the plaque I made in the Galápagos toward it. How territorial—man and his desire to leave his mark. Maybe I should just empty the trash! If I were to climb Horn Island, what would I do at the top? The same thing any animal would do—pee.

I love the hissing and the chewing cold. I like burning calories just to stay heated. I feel awake and alive.

0600. Seas eight to ten feet, rolling but generally smooth. Trouble with the steering gear with wind building to Force 8. It's a real gale, but pleasant below. Brief galley fire. Pâté, artichoke hearts, crackers, peanut butter, and chicken spread by Dad, à la floor of the cabin, for brunch.

0800–1200. Lively tiller steering—the good old days! Visibility, one-quarter mile; seas, sixteen feet, not so bad. Moving fast under triple-reefed main and full dodger.

DAY 177. Barometer easing its angle of dive. Alter course to stay north of Diego Ramirez—can't risk approaching that rock in this visibility. Will go down Drake Passage between it and The Horn, angling up to The Horn. I'm disappointed—Cape Horn is the last land mass of South America, and Diego Ramirez is just a rock, covered by cold waves and the ultimate lonely place before Antarctica. Even so, it's land.

DAY 178. On January 6, just after I got our noon position and wrote the above, a gale clomped down on us—with

Force 8 winds and gusts to Force 9. In the afternoon I came on deck and besides seeing that Dad was working hard at the tiller, the seas and sky looked furious. White streaks were smeared along the waves, the wind almost visible! Seas built and grew until it was necessary for us to look aft and steer down each wave, keeping the stern toward the following seas. Some waves were bigger than others—foaming and looking really mean. Graybeards. The automatic steering wouldn't work—the paddle was spending too much time out of the water. (The whole boat seemed to be spending too much time out of the water.) We took two-hour watches.

It's hard to see a wave (in photos, impossible). You see the mass of it—not much height—then you rise slowly as the water floods beneath you and you're on top. I was at the helm watching this really big one and suddenly I knew *Sparrow* hadn't risen and twenty feet of wave was straight up over us.

We surfed for a moment and fell off it to starboard, flat into the water. The boat didn't seem to tip over but the port rail rose up suddenly above me as I slid down. What I'd been standing on was above my shoulder level. I was in the ocean! The foaming waves I'd been looking at were at my chin. My tether was yanked tight as *Sparrow* came up level, surfed again, and fell over to port, the starboard deck and rail shooting up over my head. I kicked my legs and paddled for a moment in free water, then *Sparrow* righted and I was scooped on deck.

By the time all this happened, it had been thirty-six hours since I'd had a fix on the sun to establish our position. My dead reckoning put us near Diego Ramirez (fifty miles southwest of Cape Horn). But you can't steer accurately in a gale, so I was jumpy.

The gale broke up by 0100 and, with the moon full, there it was: a frozen wave at the end of the continent. A featureless gray hump. The Horn.

DAVID

My Horn passage started at 0700 on January 7. The sunrise had been ominous. The paddle that goes down into the water to work the self-steerer was jumping out as the stern lifted high. I jibed and the main sheet looped under the paddle, threatening to snap it off. I called for Dan and he held me by the heel like Achilles's mother as I went in headfirst for the line and cleared it. Dan was angry because I unclipped my tether, but it didn't stretch that far and I didn't want to take time to reclip it. "But we're not moving, Dan," I said weakly. I was glad he was angry because that meant he'd use the tether himself. We dismantled the Navik and steered by hand for the first time on this passage. Seas and wind built and it was a proper gale, going with us. We took in the jib; she flew with only a spot of mainsail exposed. Slocum's phrase repeated in my head: "Even while the storm raged at its worst, my ship was wholesome and noble." And *Sparrow* was magnificent: delicate but steady, swift and airy on the foam crest, strong and driving through the great valleys. She seemed born for this day.

At noon, Dan shifted course, visibility was down to a few hundred yards. Forget Diego Ramirez. If we didn't hit it we wouldn't see it. And in the slop of this gale we wouldn't see The Horn either. The Horn is three things: the rock itself, Drake Passage (the water in which you sail around it), and the whole idea of the passage. We were in the Passage, and surely we'd survive for the third. I settled for two out of three. At one that afternoon I asked Dan when we'd be off (if not crashed onto) The Horn and he said, "0100 tomorrow morning." The gale picked up and Dan steered, howling "Aaayippeeeeeee!" as we surfed down the long gray waves with their tops torn off and the spray racing us. It was quiet and dry below. I realized that Dan had hardly ever steered by tiller, but his skill was marvelous, undoubtedly honed by hours of handling the joystick in video-game parlors. He looked possessed. Horsemen have their centaurs, why don't we sailors have a name for the half-man, half-boat that Dan was at that moment?

Because we were hand-steering we changed to two-hour stints. During my early-evening watch, the gale started to fly apart, moderating. This is the most dangerous time of a gale, because the puffs can be fierce after random lulls, and the wind can shoot at you suddenly from a different direction. At eight-thirty at night I was below making tea and lighting the evening lamp when *Sparrow* went down hard to starboard. Then bam! down to port. Without a horizon below, hanging on and standing not upright but with the angle of the boat, I only knew that we were down because the water covering the porthole was not wave froth but solid green—I was looking straight down into the ocean. A felt bootliner that was drying knocked the lamp out of my hand and onto the bunk. The water roared, like a train running over us.

"OK, Dan?"

"I'm fine, Dad." His voice sounded subdued.

My eye was taken during this by the blue plastic cat pan, which was secured by cord on two sides. It jumped up, did a 180° turn and landed upside down, then leaped again and did a full 360° flip and landed face down again. It looked like a little girl in a blue dress, skipping rope. I thought of that calmly. The binoculars were in my berth with the oil lamp; their teak box had broken. It was the only thing we hadn't built ourselves. Everything else was in place. I didn't learn until he told me the next day that Dan had gone overboard.

The gale broke on my ten-to-midnight watch, and the moon, almost full, showed through the racing clouds as they tore apart: a slow film flicker. After my watch I was below, again making tea, and Dan called, "Dad, I think I see The Horn," and I was up on deck at ejection speed and there it was.

"How did you see it, Dan?"

"One wave didn't go down."

I'd never seen it but of course it was The Horn; its form must have been in my genes. The great rock sphinx, the crouching lion at the bottom of the world. The sea and the sky and the faintly outlined huge rock were all the same color—indigo, graded like the first three pulls of the same ink on a Japanese woodblock print. We embraced, then stood entranced. I went below and poured a finger of Kahlua for each of us (I oddly remembered a guest saying, "No, Leonora, the finger is held sideways, not straight down"). We toasted. I was about to say, "To the men who died here," when Dan said, "To the people who died here." It was the only possible thing to say. There was the rock, after 2,500 miles of ocean, our first sighting, the rock itself.

"You said 0100, Dan, and here we are."

"Yes, but I was aiming for ten miles off."

"You can't be less than eight . . ." I was staggered by that. Two hundred and thirty miles in thirty-six hours without sky for sights, only our eyes on the compass and on our wake to judge speed, in full gale, in strong current, and with a course change in the middle, and his error was two miles. The Horn bore north and I stepped behind him. Few had rounded The Horn in a boat this small, and he was ahead of me.

We were in the Atlantic. I had a sudden craving for simple food, and made a plain omelette for us. Three eggs in the pan, one on the floor. Perfectly moist in the middle. Just a sprinkle of dill. It was getting light. Between us and The Horn, thousands of small petrels fluttered and dipped, like a vast spread of brown-and-white lace undulating a foot above the surface.

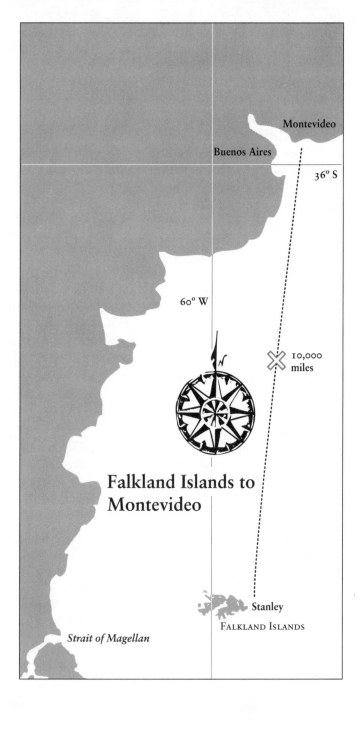

Montevideo

Buenos Aires

36° S

60° W

10,000
miles

Falkland Islands to
Montevideo

Stanley
FALKLAND ISLANDS

Strait of Magellan

10 THE TEN-THOUSANDTH MILE

For love and regret go hand in hand in a
world of changes swifter than the shifting of
the clouds reflected in the mirror of the sea.
    —*Joseph Conrad,* The Mirror of the Sea

DAN

DAY 178. Morning, January 8. There is enough light by 0300 for us to take pictures. I'm too excited to sleep. To see land after twenty-four days at sea. I'd planned to put on my wet suit and swim away to get a picture of *Sparrow* in front of The Horn, but when we are actually there the thought raises the hairs on my teeth. Dad agrees. He had thought of going up to it—I guess for forty years—and now he's too awed and wants to leave it to itself. It's not really his choice; the island won't be played with.

I had many pictures of what I thought rounding The Horn would look like. Usually *Sparrow* would be transformed into an old square-rigger and I'd be taking in the t'gallant as the seas crashed against us. But, in fact, I spend a good part of the morning annoyed that I can't get the little balls of instant milk to dissolve in my coffee.

In the Galápagos, I'd burned "Sparrow 1984" nicely into a teak board. I wanted to hang it up at Post Office Bay, but we didn't get there. I passed it up on deck before my watch, intending to throw it in the sea when we reached

The Horn. It was swept overboard when the wave threw us on our side. The sea took it.

I realize how committed I am to this boat. Last night, when *Sparrow* fell and I was in the ocean, I thought only about her, not me. If I'd been rolling over in a car I'd have thought about whether I'd live or die. But in the water I wanted to get back on board to help *Sparrow* live on. I understand that without her I'd die, and that isn't the same as a wrecked car or a burned-down house that you walk away from. But there's a deep bonding and it can turn into love and purpose. Perhaps it explains why men could live a horribly hard life on the old sailing ships. In bad storms, they would put out to sea away from the dangers of land.

I can see myself on *Sparrow* in a harbor and someone rows up and says, "Is this the *Sparrow* that went around Cape Horn?" I'll say, "Yes," and be happy that they admire the boat and won't say, "I was there too."

DAVID

By 1000, on January 8, The Horn was in clear sight behind and already we'd bent our easterly course toward north. Suddenly, a sheet of hail about the size of capers hit me so hard in the back that I stumbled forward in the cockpit. Just out of a blue sky, or at least a broken sky, not a rain or storm sky. And with it came the strongest wind we'd had, over fifty knots (Force 10). The sea stayed flat but turned white—we were already in shelter from The Horn and its islands—and in less than a minute I clawed down the jib and had another tuck in the main, and then in fifteen minutes the williwaw was over. I mostly remember the petrels chattering under the bow when I went forward. I hoped Dan wasn't awakened, but he must have heard and felt that blast of hail.

Hours later, after dinner on the day we rounded The Horn, I watched a good sunset, with clouds by Poussin, saw more seabirds (our first grebes), and the first weed in the water. It was time to read E. B. White again, and I was feeling at peace. But it breezed up and we had bumpy and crooked water by dark.

DAN

DAY 179. January 9. Mountains, just barely visible to port as we round Staten Island. They're a gray outline, and they just sit there like clouds that don't go up. Coastal navigation here with its terrors does not thrill me.

Today Tiger chewed through an electric wire and I had to replace it. I was annoyed; I plugged it in and dangled it before him until he attacked. Hairs flew in all directions and now he's hiding forward. It's been so long since I've been around normal people, I can't tell if this was cruel or smart. Anyway, we laughed, and he won't be chewing wires for a while.

DAY 180. Twenty-six days out of Easter Island, one hundred and seventy-nine days out of New London. Tiger gets his first hard-on. It passes with little ceremony except for Dad saying, "Hubba-hubba." We sail over Burdwood Bank, where the ocean floor rises from twelve hundred to thirty fathoms. The water turns Bahama turquoise, but it's not so clear that you can see bottom.

It smells like snow. A layer of wet mist covers me during the first fifteen minutes of my watch, like a newly dewed field.

DAVID

If our Horn passage had been one hour earlier, we would have shared the day that Bill Nance brought *Sparrow*'s wooden sister ship, *Cardinal Vertue,* around The Horn, exactly twenty years before, the first boat under thirty feet to make the passage. Now, two days later, I went forward to lash down a jib that had worked its way free and was billowing. I love the tiny portholes, only two inches in diameter, that we'd put in forward on the cabin sides. The one lamp from below glowed faintly through them, and all the work to make them was worth this one moment, when in the vast seascape the glow was as cozy as a Christmas Eve Currier and Ives cottage in snow. Back in the cockpit I was blowing on my fingers when suddenly my heart jumped at an eerie, flat slit of light to starboard, an orange band like a dragon's eye. Then it started to rush at us. Just like Nemo's great porthole, I thought in a flash. Heart beating fast, I realized it was the moon rising between the horizon and a black ribbon of cloud. Exactly then, there was a blood-curdling scream to port. My head swiveled around so fast that I had a sore neck for three days. An albatross, of course. A human scream indeed—there is a seaman's legend that each albatross carries the soul of a drowned sailor. Out there, as I said to Leonora—out there with Dan, yes, and with all the layers skimmed off, I had crept to the center of the intricate web of my expensive education. Alone with the vast ocean, I found far more pleasure and use for it, and far more unity with my distant fellows, than in its humdrum application of keeping afloat in the shallower waters of witty conversation at the Century Club or embassy parties.

An hour later we saw a light, our first in twenty-seven days, then another, bobbing, then another. A light at sea is hard to believe at first. It could be a nugget of phosphorescence. It drops under wave crests and is not seen steadily, so there's a long period of uncertainty and often concern. They turned out to be calamari boats; we would see them dockside in Montevideo. We sensed the land—the Falklands—that we were approaching. They were discovered in 1592, but were not settled until 1764; two big islands, about two hundred small ones. The capital town is Stanley, with a steady population of eighteen hundred. There are a couple of dozen other small settlements on the islands, a few trees, wonderful seabirds, heating by peat, and wind and more wind.

The English named the islands after the Viscount of Falkland. Also known as Islas Malvinas, the Spanish name comes from the French sailors who named the islands after their port of St. Malo. Few now remember that there was a decisive naval action here in 1914 that destroyed four German cruisers and Admiral Spee himself. It was a turning point: Britain afterward held the high seas for the Great War, challenged only in the narrow seas near home.

DAN

DAY 180. Final approach to the Falklands—dark squalls on and off all night, and I spend an exciting watch standing in the cockpit and clinging to the dodger, bending my knees, rocking and rolling with *Sparrow*. Seas build to ten feet.

I've got the usual landfall anxiety—but the sky is blue behind the squalls and there are birds all over. My concern is the current, which can set both ways, depending on the wind. I'm consuming lots of crackers and coffee, when, with very little warning, we're hit by more caper-sized hail and a gale that increases until, by 1100, Dad and I must hand-steer. Big chunks of kelp are around—which is scary because I think the land must be right under them. Lots of birds!

1200. Landfall!—a bluish hill looking like a badly painted stage backdrop. This is Cape Pembroke and on it sits an old weathered lighthouse. We round in a lather of foam. The wind is Force 8 and cold. We're down to the third reef in the main and the storm jib. It is too blowy to come about normally so we must wear ship: make a circle away from the wind and jibe. The channel here is narrow because of islands in the narrowing fairway and then tankers and troopships at anchor. It takes us four hours to zigzag the three miles to the mouth of Port Stanley, with wind gusting to Force 9! Dad finds that when he just lets go of the tiller, she sails best; the balance is perfect. The mainsail has a tiny tear—is it spreading? If it splits we'll be forced to land on the beach, which is mined. I have the anchor ready.

"Gee, Dad, the sail's tearing."

"Yeah. I don't really feel like fixing it right now, do you?"

"I'll tell you in five minutes!"

So we look at the sky through the sail and listen for the sound of popping stitches . . .

I turn on the VHF, our line-of-sight walkie-talkie, and hear the Queen's harbor master declaring a "wind warning" to all the ships about. I call him and explain that I am not familiar with the term, and did this mean that there would be *more* wind, or was he talking about *now?* He says yes, *more* wind. A military helicopter hovers by us for a while—we give him the "thumbs-up" and he waves back. Outrageous to see such high technology after so long. Harrier jets tear across the sky. The land is beautiful—harsh looking and gray.

The Queen's harbor master sends out a harbor launch, a utility boat called a *kiwi*, to pull us through the very narrow opening (dead upwind). She takes us alongside, but I see that she will scratch our hull badly, we can't fend off in this rough water. I call out to take us astern. They've got uniforms and that British nautical voice of authority, but it is our boat. They throw us a line and tow us into the cut. As we approach the harbor and the view of Stanley opens before us, the wind warning becomes a reality and *Sparrow* heels over seventy degrees with *no* sails up. Horizontal hail makes it difficult, for a moment, to distinguish land from sea from sky. The light is bright and beautiful. The roofs of the houses pile up a hill and they are many colors. The kiwi brings us along the *Forest*, an inter-island cargo ship, at dusk. Customs officers catch our lines, "Come 'round The 'Awn then 'ave you?"

We are frozen, wet, and hungry. John Reed, the development director of the island, takes us to his home for lamb curry and hot tea. It takes us about an hour to thaw, and we can hardly believe the quiet stillness of a soft couch. We've made our passage.

DAY 182. Falkland Islands. *Sparrow* is tied to a falling-apart jetty and it's calm. We were just mentioned in the local radio news—funny to hear "Daniel and David Hays" on our own radio! I've been dreaming like a video box, and my night life is full of psychological confusions— like old girlfriends dissolving or getting enlightened and waving to me as they ascend to heaven. Maybe I should get neutered.

There are live minefields here, fenced off. On the evening announcements tonight, it is said that a sheep set off an anti-tank mine and blew itself to nothing. Daily the ordinance squad finds grenades, shallow graves, and fuel casings (drop tanks) from jets. They say on the radio that they are happy to come and pick up anything found, and please not to leave it on their doorstep.

There are old half-sunken ships here, carcasses of whale ships and other Cape Horners, with tin roofs tacked on and used as warehouses. Actually, the jetty we are tied to was once a ship. We learn that in the old days, before the Panama Canal opened and when this was an important stopover, they could condemn an old ship for being unseaworthy, particularly if it had a good cargo—such as coal— that they wanted. These ship hulls became docks. They would sink them and put in enough rocks to hold them down.

When I'm by the land, I write less, and what I do write sounds like a weather report to me. Something inside me hides and doesn't want to come out even late at night when I'm alone on deck. As soon as the lines are secured to a dock, only a shell of myself is left to deal with others while my creative being dives deep. Same thing happens when I have a girlfriend. A certain wander-energy goes away.

It's a joy to speak English with people who are not Americans. Dad and I make daily excursions for supplies, and fish and chips. The local pub expects us for cider at 5:00 P.M. We hang over the bar talking about what people talk about in bars—but with a nice local-gossip twist— theories on the Falklands war, the changes since, sheep, the local brewery, deaths. There are three populations here. The old regulars, the military, and a labor group building a big new military airport so that the military can go home (with a good airport they don't have to live here). But it may not only be to do a better war next time. The rumor is that it will be a base for the Antarctica rape that will begin when current treaties expire.

The wind is usually strong and I am glad we are sheltered. Dad won another million dollars from me: he found a store that sells Superballs for Tiger. This is a small town. Dad went to the library to look up a line he's forgotten from Gilbert and Sullivan—that's the kind of furniture he has in his head and it can bug him for weeks. Anyway, the library is right at the head of the dock and when he came in the librarian looked up at him and said, "Your welding's ready."

Tough weather in the harbor. Force 8 is not uncommon in here. We have to fight to keep *Sparrow* in one piece at the dock. Yesterday the local dentist, who filled Dad's tooth, forgot to put on his parking brake and his Land Rover was blown into the harbor. It's already been rescued. The windshield is broken, but he's using it.

And then Dad wins another million! He said the English would have cat litter and he found some. And then we bet two million about cat food here and there *is* cat food. I can't believe that I even bet there wouldn't be postcards. So I'm five million behind, counting the pizza parlor, and I'll ask him for a thirty-year period to pay it off. Dad calls this a hot-air-balloon mortgage. But I refuse to give in on one of our bets. He bet there'd be a John Denver tape here (the exact language was that we could *buy* a John Denver tape) and off he goes to the local radio station where they record it for him on a cassette and he pays them a penny and now he says I owe him another million. What an investment!

The house roofs here that looked so inviting as we sailed in are brightly painted tin. There are pretty gardens, which Dad says are like English gardens; we remember our Mother Goose illustrations. We've come around South America and not been on the mainland yet. All our stops have been islands, and each has its own way of doing entertainment. In the Galápagos we went to a movie. At Easter Island all the homes were in one small village, and the Chilean government was attentive: most homes had cable television that came in over a big satellite scoop, but they got only one government station. Here in Stanley they do videocassettes. There are three little stores that rent them, and they do a big business with the military. It's an isolated life. We talk to people who grew up here: some of them want their children to grow up here too because it's pure. Most of the children want to go to England.

We have hot baths at Emma's Boarding House, and eat lamb there for dinner. It's all lamb and mutton here. We meet the vet, who's living there, and he says that he saw Tiger on the dock and if he sees that happen again, he'll have to put him away because they're terrified of animal disease here. They don't have any. If they get hoof-and-mouth disease, their sheep will be wiped out, and that's their living.

We are carrying a lot of spare teak and some plywood for emergencies, but no pine. We buy some and Dad makes a ceiling about two feet square to cover the raw fiberglass in the vestibule area, just forward of the mast. *Sparrow*, he says, is almost done. A few other yachts come in during the week. One is a German fifty-foot steel boat with a father and two sons. This is their first landfall since the Galápagos. As they rounded Cape Horn they passed within a half-mile of a boat going the other way, a boat they knew from their hometown! There is something I like about Germans—a sort of harshness that is very direct. When I was talking about maybe getting Tiger "fixed" (broken is more like it), the father said, "*No!* You can't take that away from him, he will be dead—a stupid thing that eats . . . so he stinks up the house a little, it is a very manly smell."

Another yacht, the thirty-one-foot *Gigi*, is on her second trip around The Horn from east to west. Her captain is Ty Techera, who only just learned to sail within the last two years. "My daughter wanted me to take a class with her . . ." His ignorance is refreshing. It has nothing to do with not knowing — it has to do with him not having all these fixed ideas about sailing. Why *not* the harder way around The Horn? Why not alone? He's also a joy to be around because, unlike many sailors I've met, he doesn't interrupt the boring sea story I'm telling with the usual boring story of his own. He listens.

I believe his trip is sponsored by the National Oceanic and Atmospheric Administration, the United States Coast Guard, *National Geographic,* and a few others. He has their logos sewn on his sail. Dad says it looks like an old theater advertising curtain. Below it's full of machines that beep and burp, including a special box that he will throw over the side if a Russian ship stops him. Maybe we could have had sponsors too, but we lied and didn't say that we were going around The Horn.

DAY 192. On my birthday we give a dinner for Ty and for the manager of the brewery here, Ron. There is even a cake, and it's pleasant. It was spoiled a bit for Dad when Ron said "Jew-boy" in the course of conversation. I didn't hear it. Dad says that's very British: they have more deeply built-in bigotry than even we have at home; they say these things without thinking, as a part of the language.

DAY 193. Awake 0430. Ty comes down at 0500 and we all have a messy goodbye omelette and talk. Easy to kick up our feet, we've done everything now and are invincible — but any voyage has its dark clouds and I feel anxiety. I'm scared for Ty, going the wrong way around The Horn. He has a big iron frame (looks like a roll bar) in his cockpit to hold the radar and I don't think it's safe. But his sense of humor is too good for him to die. We lend Ty our *Aku Aku* and urge him to go to Easter Island. The book will go around The Horn both ways, we hope.

Into the Atlantic again. In the outer harbor we have an escort of king penguins. They are very much like porpoises, but only two or three feet long. They jump out of the water in exactly the same way, but in a smaller and faster arc, and make *pthsss* sounds, sucking in air.

After two weeks ashore we are both seasick in short sloppy seas. I throw up nineteen times. Dad says he isn't seasick, just disgusted watching me throw up, so he does too, and then for some reason can't stop. We're weak as puppies but Dad crawls forward and takes down the jib and backs the forestays'l so we can heave to and just lie quietly for the night. "Heroic," I say when he crawls back. He says, "Stupid word," and vomits. We've learned in Stanley that Cape Horners can pee to windward and are allowed to put their feet up on the table in the officers' wardroom in an English warship.

DAY 195. Miserably sick again, after my "I can't believe I have to eat this" pancakes. Small egg accident in the fo'c'sle leaves an awful smell. After only fifty hours at sea, my first sun fix is six miles off, but I'm happy.

Sailing just on the edge scares me. We are in fog at night, oppressive and mysterious. The genoa pulls us at five knots, heeled *just* down to the decks, tensing, not willing to get us wet enough to reduce to the #1 jib but tempting — and in the white, thick darkness, who knows what's a hundred feet ahead? This part of the journey is strange to me. Ahead is the first mainland since Panama three months ago and Dad will go home. It's only a thousand miles, which at this point is just a yawn.

Tiger and I are so cool—he'll jump in from the hatch, landing expertly on the foul-weather-gear bin. I'm leaning against it, writing and wearing headphones, and I feel him thump land. I immediately turn to touch noses with him. "Getting any?" he asks. "Yah, as much as you!" He turns and goes off to cat fantasy.

DAY 197. Gad, am I sick! Food poisoning? Dad takes my watch. I thank him and he's so pleased to take care of me again. So much for the "continuous meal" theory.

DAY 198. We are out of the south circle—July weather, but it's colder. Yesterday was the first naked day in over two months, white shrively bodies. I still have short hair—too short to comb or brush. I'm twenty-five now, and this year I'm gonna meet a great Jewish-Italian Southern girl. Gawd. Still sick. Each fart is a risk.

As we head north again, the stars become more familiar—but not till I see the North Star at about 10° north (in 3,600 miles) will *Sparrow* be what I consider "north" again. Today she sailed her ten-thousandth mile, and Tiger and I have been on board for all of it. I've been creaming Dad in gin—daily scores like 175 to 42, but overall he's ahead, 3,742 to 3,021. But he cheats—leaves off points of mine when he's doing scores. (I change them when he's asleep.)

DAVID

Dear Leonora,

Dan and I had a big fight today. I guess it wasn't a fight. I talked excitedly, Dan just listened and afterward I think he cried, I went up on deck so he could. I'm sure he didn't cry—if he did—because of the fight, but because of love. And I didn't really yell. It's been storing up. I said that I was tired of being seen as goddam old and one of my biggest wishes was that when he gets to my age he can be as strong and do as much and it's not fair to call me senile or think that I am and so what if I can't always find stuff maybe he's not the only one on this boat with a lot of things going on in his head.

Then I said that I *am* going to die and I'm at peace with the idea and it feels just great being my age and a little decrepit. That's one reason I was *with him* as my best friend and companion but he wasn't my best friend he's my son dammit and they're different things and furthermore I'm planning to die before he does unless he does some stupid daredevil stuff like—I couldn't think of anything—and he just better get used to that idea. Because if he died first I'd only survive him for five minutes and don't forget it because that's the way generations go and he can carry all the baggage he wants about my death because I carry it around about my dad. But one damn thing he'll never have to tote is that I didn't do all the terrific things in life that *I* wanted to do, the way *my* dad didn't. And Dan's made them twice, ten times, as good for me. And, back on the subject (I may have yelled a bit here), I wasn't that damn old and I'm doing just fine and blah blah blah.

He said, "Dammit, Dad, you always have to be right," but I was ready for him and I said, "And dammit, Dan, you've arranged your life so you can never be wrong." I really did mean what I said, but it's not so bad, he knows it. Then I said that I knew he was a better sailor but that's not because I was old, it's just because he had such a damn good teacher and he has such good instincts and anyway I didn't start to sail until I was nine. And then I said he was a better human being too and I hope he believes me because it's true. Love, David

I was dismayed and uncertain about what I'd done. The voyage was at the right time in my life. I could only guess that it was right for Dan. Should I have so quickly made him our captain? It would have been inevitable anyway.

Well, we talked more, and I learned something. In the back of a sea boot at the top there's usually a little grommet, I guess so you can put a string through to hang them up. Our boots were the same brand and almost the same size, his, a half size larger. It was important that we each cared for our own gear. So I put little cords through the grommets of my boots to distinguish them from his in the dark. Then, because boots are loose enough and the right/left is subtle but annoying if they're wrong, I tied two knots in the right boot, one in the left. Now, this simple mnemonic never seemed to work, and it did indeed worry me that I was losing it upstairs and could never remember it correctly. On they'd go—left on right. Dan now told me that as a practical joke he's been changing the knots every week. We howled with laughter. He said that he thought I'd be more upset, and he was sorry he did it because of what I had just said. I said yes, it caused me a lot of worry but now I remembered our number-one rule, The Big Rule, or BR, that if you're going to laugh about something in six months or a year, you might as well start laughing now. That's when I went up on deck so that he could think and maybe cry, because of all the junk I said, he'd pull out the one idea that I was going to die. But how could I be dead while he's still living? An old sophistry? No, not any longer. Now, to me, a reality. I'm surprised at how real it is, how true and simple. (Later, when I told this story about the boots to Julia, she said I should have retaliated by changing his watches a half-second so they didn't "meep" at the same time.)

When I took "est," there was a section of the training when, tired and hungry, you put your head between your knees and listened to the trainer incant this and that, and you felt ready to deal with matters that haunted you and could shed an old skin. I ran down the list in my mental warehouse, thought of dealing with a dishonest man I despised but discarded that as a waste of a good opportunity—and that decision itself exorcised that small but nagging problem. Then I thought I'd deal with the sadness I still felt after twenty-two years because my father was not around. It catches me hard, two or three times a year, so suddenly and so hard that I sit and cry, real tears. But I decided not to deal with that. Why should I? It's clear, it's fresh and clean, and it's simple. I miss him. That's all. Crying for him is one of my best things; I want it.

DAN

DAY 200. First light. A big swell from the east with a reddish sunrise.

I can't find Tiger: he's not on board.

I'm churned up by the picture of him in the cold ocean watching *Sparrow* sail away. A black shape in the night, which he's never seen from that angle before. How long did he swim? Did he understand?

Dear Mom,

Gloomy day—last night, Tiger fell overboard and all day my head's been full of images of him—there's this vacuum where he was—there's no meowing, purring, cuddling, or playing. So many things in that sweet fur. He's been on for ten thousand miles exactly, so I guess he was a ten-thousand-mile cat—one thousand miles for each life and one extra because he was so loving.

Dismal. I usually find a good side to all shitty things—like in a gale, at least it won't get worse; with a flat tire you get to check out your spare, etc., but here, not much comes up. Mortality sucks. Love, Dan

DAVID

Tiger was gone. And I heard the splash! I came below about eleven at night. We were on deck more now in warmer weather and we were more alert as we came into shipping lanes. Tiger had been doing what Dan calls his evening "spaz run," leaping at coils of line along the rail. The rail has two lifelines, thin wires, at waist and knee height, good for a sailor but nothing for a cat. When I came below, I heard the splash, but there are so many splashes on a boat, so many noises, and we were moving briskly, and I quickly and lightly rationalized it away. Did the name Tiger even come to mind? It must have or I wouldn't have remembered at all. Dan comforted me because we couldn't have done anything, or even seen the tiny white face in the foam. Or else we would have done something stupid like jump in, and that could have been worse.

Maybe a bird came near, or a flying fish, and he sprang. Or he just missed his coil, or misstepped from a perilous place where he liked to lie. He should have had a tether, too. We photographed him on his last day, coiled in a line, and I made Dan laugh by performing a magic show and pulling him out of my hat. Now our little witness was gone; Tiger, who stretched out to touch your nose to his every time you were near. Dan was stoic but heartbroken. Tiger's whole world was here, his whole life, and now so much of ours. I thought, well, it wasn't Dan or me, and I almost said it, but realized just in time that that would have been the stupidest thing I could have said during the entire voyage. We had nothing to do. No little pet grave to dig. We emptied the pan of litter.

It was February 1; I had twenty-eight days left of my sabbatical and the next day was my father's birthday.

DAN

DAY 201. Today we spent another two hours on The Knot. This tangle was once a six-hundred-foot spool of white quarter-inch nylon. The cardboard discs at the end of the spool fell off, so now it's literally six hundred feet of knot. This is our third day working on it. We take turns. Bright noon, misty cold winds.

The cat. I still stick my head up through the hatch and go "Mrrow?" No answer. We failed him. He came to us directly from his mother. He never experienced anything outside our small world. He was on a dock only twice. We should have dunked him in the uncomfortable water. He never knew that an inch outside the shell of his world there was no help, and fast and certain death. I think of Andrea, a girlfriend who drowned when the *Marquesa* sank near Bermuda. When I was little and lost something overboard, Julia told me that Poseidon's little boy probably didn't have a toy like mine and now he did—I stopped crying. I hope that Tiger has found Andrea.

DAY 202. We spent the night rolling in fog, floating in the black. This thousand-mile run to Montevideo is taking a long time. We were told it could be stormy or take three weeks—or both. Finally, a northwest breeze comes up. As the sun rises we slide along at over four knots. Birds come to check us out.

DAY 204. We are at the Río de la Plata, a big estuary with Buenos Aires all the way in and Montevideo in the northeastern part. First we smell land—not quite smoke or exhaust, but a sort of thickness, which has not been present since October in Panama. You need big cities and their people to generate this kind of pollution. The water is also different—it seems thicker. At 1030 we see a moth, at 1045 a dragonfly. By 1100 we see a vague cluster of pencil shapes in wobbly heat-air—Montevideo. Flies on board by 1200. And by 1500 we are anchored at the yacht club ("yache cloob") in a harbor that is a hot, sticky, smelly, fly-buzzing cesspool.

DAY 205. I walk the streets of Montevideo like an alien to the human race—I am really frightened of contact.

Lonely—no, empty—not having Tiger to greet us on our return from daily excursions. I walk around in a trance. Unable and unwilling to really "communicate" with locals—though I do well in a sort of pantomime. Dad loves it. At sea I'm the captain; ashore with him, I tag along in a familiar father–son role.

DAY 210. When we got here I said to Dad that if we stumbled on a new cat, OK, but I won't look for one—leave it to destiny. Two days later Dad tripped and almost fell over a black-and-white, blue-eyed, six-week-old kitty, one of five born to a gray momma living in the yacht club's garbage dump. We couldn't find him the next day—he kept himself apart. We found him two days later and pulled off gobs of fleas and ticks during his first bath. He looked very miserable. With a flea collar, a worm pill, and ear-mite medicine, he was like a newly innoculated immigrant.

I walk five miles of beaches.

DAVID

Here's a note for sailors: a wedge of cheese is excellent to keep cans from rattling, but don't forget where you wedged it. Once I cleaned up the mess, I told Dan some wonderful flying dreams I'd been having. They'd been recurring. Dan was not convinced that they recur. He explained to me that the mind is in full control of a dream, and can therefore create for you the false belief that you've been there before. Dan has disciplined himself to wake up after a dream, write it down, and then easily go back to sleep.

Walking through Montevideo, I felt a European grace, a

quality from the immigrants who settled here—a touch of Paris, Barcelona, Lisbon. We phoned home. We pigged out on junk food and saw bad movies. I got a haircut, the first one in five years that my daughter, Julia, hadn't given me, except for Leonora's on Easter Island. The barber was Hungarian, like Leonora. I bought sneakers and took a taxi back to the boat. The driver told me the fare to the harbor. It seemed high, but I said OK. He was a German immigrant. His father ran an opera company before the war.

"Berlin?" I asked. He nodded.

"Did you know Lena Abarbanell?"

"Oh yes, as a child."

Lena was brought to New York to originate the role of Hansel at the Met. She became the most famous "Merry Widow." We were close to her in her last years. Talk of theatre friends, conversations in taxis: unmistakable signs I was coming back to land. When we arrived at the dock the fare was only half what he had stated. "Why?" I asked. He turned and looked straight at me, "I wanted to be sure you *really* wanted to go."

We bought some good, thin teak, and on my last day I covered the plain plywood surface of the vegetable bin we built in Panama. *Sparrow* was finally completed. And I was leaving. Later, Dan came with me to the airport and we didn't say much because it had all been said. I walked as usual, with my hand on his shoulder, and it seemed to me that he was a bit taller than he was before the voyage. He had been an inch taller than me, but now perhaps he was an inch and a half, and when he came home we checked this and yes, he did grow that much.

Dan said he had trouble expressing his love for me. I told him he was wrong, he didn't really hide it well. We said goodbye and hugged. I said, "Good sailing," and I kept my shoulders from shaking as I walked straight away.

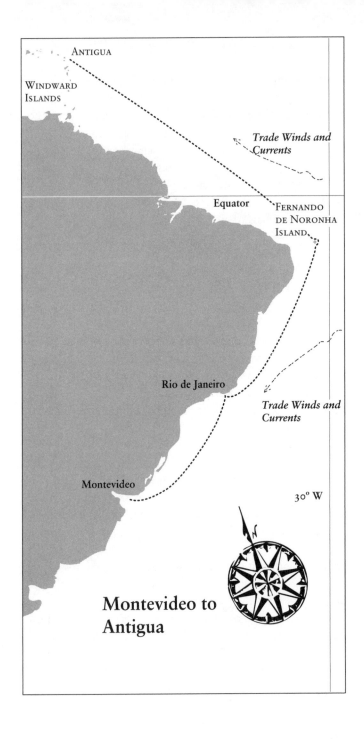

ANTIGUA

WINDWARD
ISLANDS

*Trade Winds and
Currents*

Equator

FERNANDO
DE NORONHA
ISLAND

Rio de Janeiro

*Trade Winds and
Currents*

Montevideo

30° W

N

Montevideo to
Antigua

11 Forty-two Days

It isn't that life ashore is distasteful to me. But
life at sea is better.
  —*Sir Francis Drake*, Letters

DAN

DAY 216. I'm glad he's gone. With him here I'm a kid, and even though I captain the boat I look to him as Daddy and it's hard being grown with a daddy in earshot. When I'm alone I can act like I'm unique and sprang from thin air, instead of seeing where I came from, being in a shadow.

It's a cold, silent row out to *Sparrow*. A bottle of wine I broke aboard spilled into the bilge, and it smells sour. I sleep so lightly with the new cat—like a lover—I wake at any murmur.

DAY 217. I watch my second-favorite pen vanish down the hole of a squat toilet—to reach in after it would require four times the determination it took to sail around The Horn.

DAY 221. Joe arrives! We went to college together. Great excitement, talking madly at each other and lusting after the girls. Joe admits they're better than his girls in Arizona.

Together we're like two guys in Kerouac's *On the Road*. Joe has saved for a year to join me for this homeward journey.

DAY 228. We sail at 0530, after doing those final things like stowing the rubber boat deep in the aft compartment. Feels stormy.

DAY 229. Joe's second letter to God:

Dear God,

The first letter didn't get much response, so I'm writing another. If there's any small promise I could make you in exchange for not being seasick, like cutting off my legs or never having sex again, just mention it and I'll be happy to do it.

This isn't easy. Humbly yours, Joe

DAY 230. Joe's still sick. It's typical: his first sail ever and we're in a near gale for three days straight, beating to windward and pounding like crazy. I made good chicken soup tonight—the first anything he's eaten in two days . . .

DAY 232. Gale all day.

DAY 236. The wind is so soft I think the moonlight is pushing us, filling the sails with silvery ghost breath. The new cat makes a lot of noise when you step on him. His worst habit is sliding down a leg or an arm with his claws out to slow him down, leaving skid marks all the way. Gurgling, white foam trails behind and a small pilot fish swims along just under the bow near the surface, moving exactly in rhythm with the boat, truly as if it were towing us.

DAY 243. We slosh all day long in light air just twenty miles from land. As the sun sets, we are intimidated by a huge statue of Christ, lit up on top of one of the mountains around Rio de Janeiro, but seeming to float in the sky. Not until sunset does the land breeze whisper in our sails. We blow ashore and into a small yacht basin. A man in a launch comes out and gives us some peanuts while talking Portuguese to Joe's Spanish. I did almost as well with my pantomime. We inflate the dinghy and get ashore, find various health officials and legal types and showers, and then get into a taxi, complete with whorehouse brochures.

DAY 244. Rio. Joe will fly home from here. He's been seasick for thirteen days and doesn't seem on the brink of getting well. Probably like Pavlov's dog, he'll never be able to separate the feelings of nausea, dizziness, and depression from sailing. I'll finish alone. I'm worried about my mom worrying. Will enough ships report me? Can I spend two months alone? Physically—yes. Mentally? The idea appeals to me, though it's no great practice for communication. I will have to write. Or go mad. I've never been a *month* talking to no one.

DAY 247. Joe and I spend hours wandering through Rio. The city is full of those clouded New York faces, yet you can look people in the eye and smile. We see a monkey on a man's shoulder. His body, tucked in, is the size of a large grade A egg, and his tail is ten inches long. The creature oozes fear. I fall immediately in love. Fifteen minutes and thirty dollars later he's on my shoulder, clinging to my collar with one hand and my earlobe with the other. Now I'll have two nonhuman buddies for the long voyage back.

DAY 249. I put Joe in a cab to the airport.

I just tried calling Dad, who's back in Connecticut. I want to speak to him before I go off. It's so odd to me—I am far away yet cannot think of not calling first, making sure my family is at ease with a long solo voyage.

Sparrow's ready. I just need some bread and monkey food, and . . .

I give in. I go to buy a dirty magazine. I am nervous, like a kid trying to buy his first rubber. They are displayed here in big sheets—maybe twenty-five magazines all clothespinned together. I quietly touch the *Penthouse* and sort of whisper, "This one," and the whole mass of them leaps free and crashes all over the sidewalk. It takes three guys to recover them from a small crowd of onlookers.

DAY 250. I'm on the town waiting to be picked up by a hooker. I've always wanted to try this, and just to make sure I'd go through with it, I promised Joe, before he left, that I'd do it. I'm armed with two condoms that fell out of a friend's knapsack two years ago when he visited *Sparrow* under construction—they've been frozen solid during two winters, and moved from locker to shelf to drawer. Now they are in my pocket.

I go to one of the fancy bars advertised by the cab drivers—they must get a kickback of some sort because the cab driver I met earlier is also at the bar, claiming me as his catch and talking with the headwaiter (probably a tuxedoed pimp).

The bar is full of foreigners with a smorgasbord of prostitutes. Some dance to the American disco music onstage, some mingle (one just threw a peanut at me, winking), and some dance nude to keep the air charged. The beer saturates my brain and the girls get prettier. Eventually, a princess walks by. I reach out and touch her. She tells me a hundred dollars. I say, "A hundred dollars! You're joking, right?" She walks away, which is the surest way to get me interested.

Taxi, row out to *Sparrow*. We talk. She's saving money to visit her boyfriend in Italy. She is hungry; I feed her Pepsi, bread, and cheese. She smells wonderful. Small breasts and a muscular ass, white panties that look like a balled-up knot of string on the cabin floor. Sex like happy puppies, during which I must continuously pull the cat and monkey off of us. Both seem curious and interested. We are the beast with four backs.

At 0430 I put her in a taxi. The guards at the gate wink and giggle as I pass them. I'm all satisfied and feel good to have done this—a fantasy is terrific to fulfill because it makes room for new ones. I sleep for an hour and wake up with a milk-curdling hangover and notice my wallet is missing. But then I'm not angry—it's her job to get money from men. Any "intimacy" is purely my own creation; she didn't violate any bond.

Telegram to my father: "Wallet stolen by mediocre whore. Cancel Mobil, Texaco, and MasterCard."

DAY 251. *Out, out, out!* I'm solo, except for the monkey and the cat, sloshing out into the harbor and towing a yellow polypropylene line to catch me if I fall in. I also promised Dad I'd wear my harness the whole time.

Monkey is trying to eat my blood-soaked bandage. It happened the day after the hooker's visit—I sliced off the tip of my finger with a razor. When I did the "est" training in 1982 I realized why I had so many accidents—why at twenty-two I'd cut myself seriously at least once a year and had over one hundred stitches and scars all over my body. When I was three years old and playing on the floor by Mommy, she left me to answer the phone. I sat there unhappily, feeling rejected and lonely. I had a little knife, with which I had been cutting up old letters that I'd spilled out of the garbage can, and I stabbed my right index finger with it. I howled and got blood all over, but most importantly Mom came running. Thereafter a pattern formed, and I spent much time in hospital emergency wards. Each injury was a unique "accident." I realized that when I smashed a cola bottle in one hand, I was reaching to kiss Becky for the first time with the other. When I jumped from the dock to my motorboat and missed, cutting open my shin, I was trying to impress my soon-to-be girlfriend. The list goes on, and each time I thought I was in danger of *not* being loved. It's been years now since I've had a stitch. Maybe if I hadn't done "est" I'd have another fifty impressive scars.

The voyage alone is dreamlike. The monkey screams at a very annoying frequency, piercing and upsetting, until I turn a bowl over on top of him and he goes to sleep.

DAY 253. *Sparrow* sails toward these huge orange glows in the sky, which eventually resolve themselves into flames. By dawn I am among many oil platforms—burning off gas that shoots hundreds of feet into the sky. I count fourteen platforms, seven tankers, three tugboats, and a helicopter, a city of greasy hard work.

Falling over would be horrible. To watch *Sparrow* sail away in a straight line, while I, two hundred miles offshore, prepare to live as long as I can swim—I get the shivers thinking of it. Sailing alone is hard because it's difficult to set into a rhythm or a routine. I don't eat regularly or sleep at specific times. It is easy to get lethargic—sometimes I sleep fourteen hours a day.

I'm making sail for Fernando de Noronha, about fifteen hundred miles away. This is an island six by two miles with a Brazilian military outpost. I'll stop there and phone home. Surging with freedom, I yell at clouds, cheer sunrises, chase the cat around deck, and generally follow any impulse. I'm just a tube through which impulses pause for earthy expressions. Very happy to oblige! Until, that is, I slip and fall in monkey shit. I'm angry until the monkey runs across the stove and burns the hair off his tail.

As I'm putting away a chart, a cockroach staggers to the middle of the floor (not easy to stagger with six legs), turns over, kicks twice, and dies. I meet my third crew member at his funeral. Crash (the cat) eats him.

Eventually, I give *The Brothers Karamazov* another try. At page six, after meeting just eight characters with names that thoroughly confuse me, like a phone book with hiccups, I quit. (But I did read the Grand Inquisitor section.) I shave with the monkey hanging upside down from my razor. Sailing through a school of one-inch-long flying fish—they all take off together out of one big wave, and it looks like thousands of pins falling down a blue marble stairway. I spend an hour watching the bow wave, a forever curl of motion. I open a coconut and Crash goes crazy. He leaps at it and hangs by his teeth from a piece in my hand. I give him a third and he drags it off.

Some nights I'm up every hour changing sails—reefs, storm sails, jibs, full sail, big jibs. One morning I converse with rotting onions—not very deep conversation, you understand. I quote some Vonnegut to them:

> We are here for no purpose, unless we can invent one.
> Of that I am sure. The human condition in an
> exploding universe would not have been altered one
> tenth if, rather than live as I have, I had done nothing
> but carry a rubber ice-cream cone from closet to closet
> for sixty years.

DAY 265. Yahoo! I speak to a ship bound for Egypt, or maybe from Egypt, and he says he'll send a cable home for me.

I've been wearing my harness all the time and I hate it, feeling like a tangle. Yesterday, I raised myself a quarter of the way up the mast by accident. I laughed, then let go of the line and fell to the deck, surprised. A school of dolphins accompanied us for four hours last night. Uphill, uphill we go, into the wind and current. I can hardly wait to pass Fernando de Noronha—the easternmost point of Brazil, just south of the equator—hang a left, and then all the sailing is downwind, and I fucking deserve it. It's been all left turns since Panama. This last thousand miles has been in the Doldrums, with what wind there is pushing me against the coast.

I have a dream that I come home and this old girlfriend hands me a baby, saying, "Here, it's yours."

At sunset, I yawn, and the monkey leaps into my mouth. As I pull him out by the tail he "goes Velcro." My mouth is tingly inside.

DAY 270. Twenty-one days out. I've been alone these past twenty-one days and I realize that of all the voices in my mind, the ones I really loathe remain silent! The one that says, "How do I look? And am I being cool enough? Different enough?" That one simply isn't there anymore. Back home, I don't see people as the miracles they are, and I don't see myself as the miracle I am. Instead, I try to run up an incredible resume to prove that I'm OK.

Two hundred and eight miles upwind is Fernando. In the last two days I've sailed just forty miles. Now there's no wind at all. I sleep hours at a time on deck under the stars. It's hot, and I listen to lots of AM radio. I collect rainwater when I can—almost all the tanks are full now. A school of tuna leaped about yesterday, boinging out of the water like watermelon pits squeezed between fingers. I snorkled yesterday and cleaned all the barnacles and weeds off the hull. It hasn't been painted since Panama, so the poisons in the paint are running thin, and lots of sea creatures are easily attached. The water is so clean I can see the scraped-off barnacles raining down for about one hundred feet. I find I'm uncomfortable not being attached to *Sparrow*—I can't go more than ten feet away without extreme anxiety, even though there is no wind and the sail is on deck. I dive as far as I can and look up at my world. My lungs burn and I go back.

I've been listening to too much "Voice of America." I

wake one morning at 0300 from my sleep on deck in a gentle breeze, and I find myself in dream haziness thinking, "Those goddamn *Russians*, how long can they keep it up with this piddly wind?"

The monkey runs up the mast and for two hours clings to the flagstaff at the tippy top, swinging and literally fluttering with the flag. I have to lower the flag to retrieve him, and he's fluffy when I do. Now I must teach him to change light bulbs—one of them is burned out up there. Crash eats another flying fish; there are scales and eyeballs all over. He nuzzles for a kiss and breathes fish guts in my mouth. We're not getting on. He's an OK kitten, but there are too many memories, comparisons to Tiger. It was just too soon. I'll give him away at my next port.

My profound boredom is suddenly interrupted by a distant disturbance on the water toward which I am slowly sailing. It becomes hundreds, maybe four hundred, porpoises in a group. A freight train–sized school, just leaping into the air—some straight up ten feet—and who knows what is going on below (they're very busy down there, too). Then they all turn together and race off full speed, so there are at least fifty in the air at each moment. It sounds like surf.

DAY 272. The Big Dipper tonight for the first time! It's beautiful and upside down but still pointing to the North Star, which I won't see till I'm over the equator and then some. That will be thrilling, to be back in the Northern Hemisphere. I cheer for five minutes. Orion's been visible the whole time, but the Big Dipper! I want to get home. "You guys, that's it, that's the thing I've been talking about. You see it?" The monkey looks up, the cat farts.

DAY 273. 2200—There it is—Fernando de Noronha! I see the lighthouse, bright. The skies cleared and yes, naturally, the wind is dying, so I'm slogging. I'm excited about trying to signal the radio station. I hope someone listens to the marine frequencies. I have all my mail in a waterproof bag in case I can't land and meet a fisherman and can throw it to him.

DAY 274. Up at 0400 and I set sail for the lighthouse, still twenty miles north. It's a quiet morning, though I did hit the one thunderstorm in the area. I approach in such readiness! Wearing shorts, with *Sparrow* all tidy above and below, my camera loaded, my binoculars out, my hair combed, signal flags ZD2 up ("Report me to Lloyd's"), VHF radio ready, chart on deck . . . Also the sealed pouch with the letters and an envelope marked "Commandante," with a note inside asking him to send a telegram or make a collect call for me.

Today marks the last corner of *Sparrow*'s voyage—the farthest north is Fishers Island, farthest west is Easter Island, farthest south is Horn Island, and now the farthest east is Fernando. That leaves about 2,100 miles to Antigua, where Julia and Jack will join me for more island hopping. Glenn will relieve them at St. Thomas for the passage to Bermuda. It's around 3,360 miles to home. I'm clearly past the Doldrums—should have fair wind from now on.

I smell earth! It's a dry, piney flavor I want to eat. The wind blows from the small piece of land. I half-circle the island and the wind is still in my teeth, dead against me for 180°! Maybe that's where all the wind in this part of the world is manufactured. Maybe someone there doesn't want me. This rock is jagged and lonely looking. An ominous squall blows up. It sits over the island and the wind is against me, and . . .

I don't stop. It is good to be aimed out again. I watch the island fading and wonder what it was like on land there and if I'll ever see the island again. I realize what I am afraid of. Meeting people, trying to talk to them. The squall that sits there seems like a pretty good metaphor for life ashore. I turn from it, laughing, and look ahead.

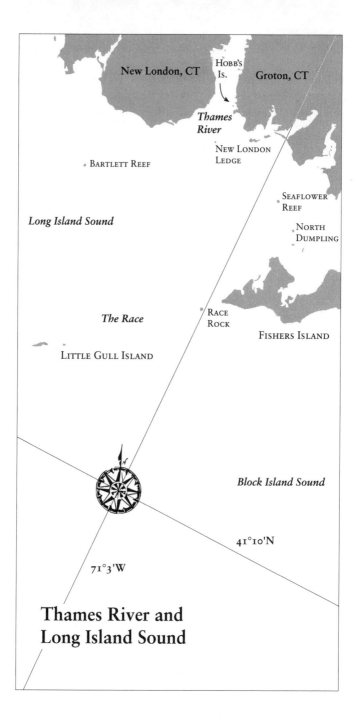

New London, CT HOBB'S Is. Groton, CT

Thames River

NEW LONDON LEDGE

• BARTLETT REEF

SEAFLOWER REEF

NORTH DUMPLING

Long Island Sound

The Race

RACE ROCK

FISHERS ISLAND

LITTLE GULL ISLAND

Block Island Sound

41°10'N

71°3'W

Thames River and Long Island Sound

12 Looking Seaward

A man who is not afraid of the sea will soon be drowned . . . for he will be going out on a day when he shouldn't. But we do be afraid of the sea, and we do only be drowned now and again.

—*John M. Synge,* The Aran Islands and Other Writings

DAVID

The terns have come for their summer stay at our island. They arrive on May 2 every year, usually in the afternoon, flying in out of the sun when it is in the southwest. Perhaps not every year. In the last ten that I have logged them, once they came in on May 3, and for two years, including this year, I was unable to bring out my office work and wait for them. I calculate I'm here three days late. They're tough little birds and beautiful flyers with their deep wing beats. I caught one at night five years ago, casting for bass off the south rock of the island. He dove for the lure. I tried to reel in to free him, but he was so aflutter at the end of the line that I cut it and hoped he could rub the hook from his beak.

Four or five pairs of terns will settle on this half-acre of rock with its dab of beach. They make no nest; the two or three dappled eggs are placed on the sand or on a flat spot of rock. The terns share the space with three pairs of mute swans, a pair of mallards, some sparrows that nest under the dock or in the big beach rosebush, and a starling that nests in the core of a wire reel that floated in and is used as an outdoor table. The swans will rush at you hissing if you go too close, but the terns take to the air and scream and dive. The ferocity of attack is at its height when the chicks are young, because the terns fear the black-backed gulls who will carry away a tern chick before it can fly. A stroke of the tern's tiny, sharp talons will make your scalp bleed, but with seemingly human ingenuity and more charm they can loose a blob of tern shit that hits with astonishing accuracy and an impact that can stagger you. Hard hats float to the island from nearby factories and shipyards, and we wear them at nesting time, but these birds can aim their bombs at your ears, even under the rim of a hat.

Full protective frenzy has not begun, but the couples are already restless and jockeying for their nesting places, chattering and diving. They seem annoyed that they've come home for the summer and I'm here again.

From the upper windows of this house Dan and I built together you can see the lights of North Dumpling, New London Ledge, New London Light, Race Rock, and Montauk, which are the big lighthouses he sailed past on his way out almost ten months ago. Last night I didn't sleep, but watched the stars circle. I came out here to be alone because I cannot maintain the confidence I've been showing to Leonora. Dan is overdue. It's been forty-one days since Joe left him and I got his telegram. One message came in soon after he left Rio, but it was garbled and I couldn't trace the vessel that sent it, or I would have known Dan's position from the track of the big ship. By my estimates, Dan should have arrived ten days ago. Only ten days, and winds, currents, I know, I know. I phoned the Coast Guard to ask about sea searches, but the area is too vast. The officer was not deterred; he wanted to help, but my throat closed and I couldn't speak, and he understood that. Over my long silence he told me to phone back anytime. Maybe I will. It's too early.

There are still pirates, and other things can happen, but the image that I am obsessed with is the hull going by, the last grab and miss. I can see with the eye at water level the rail of the boat so suddenly high and the slick leaping surface of the hull. The reach up—gone! I can hear in my mind the swish/gurgle of the stern and rudder flashing by. The one grab, and then as he turns, *swisssh*, and the trailing line is by, so much sooner than he expected. I see a beautiful bright blue sky, the puffy white trade-wind clouds. He rises and falls gently in soft, round waves.

One grab, that's what I see. That's all I've seen these past weeks, and I taught him, I caused this, I sent him, a horrifying Daedalus. I've never believed that I could outlive either of my children. What I would do, how my own life would end, I don't know.

I'm up with first light. A day-trip fishing boat, the *Hellcat* out of Groton, passes every morning at 6:20 A.M., and I know her and the other regulars, the ferries, each by their engine sound, even by the particular sound and spacing of their wakes striking the sheer west rocks of the island. While we were away, winter shorebirds came into the house through a window that broke loose, and I clean the feathers from Dan's sleeping loft. I walk on the rocks, and I sit and look seaward. There is a tideline on the island, and I pick up the seaweed and driftwood that I find there, lest they smother the shore grass that holds together our patch of sandy soil. The task seems utterly pointless to me now. And then there is a screech, and, in a burst of beaten air, I feel a streak of small sharp pain. The tern flies off, rises steeply, and swings around to look at me. She hovers almost like a hummingbird. My hand goes up to my bald spot, the avian bull's-eye. I see a dab of blood on my fingers.

"Relax, it will be all right. Easy, Mother, I won't hurt your babies." And I realize that I will live on, if it must be without Dan, or Julia. I've never loathed myself as much.

I go ashore and drive to the office. The phone rings, and a musical Caribbean voice asks me to accept a collect call from a Captain Ahab in Antigua.

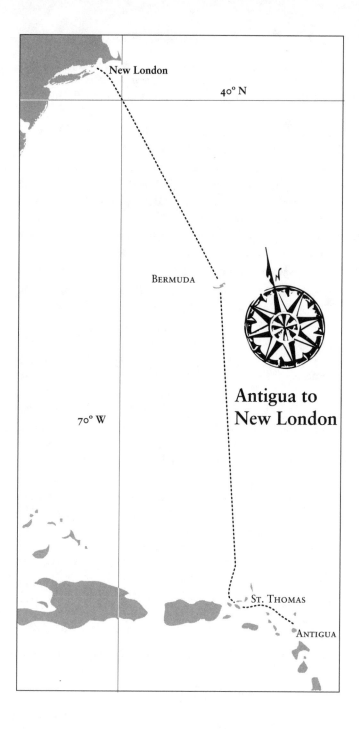

13 HOME

"You man come 'lone?"

"Yes."

"I don't believe that. You had other mans,
and you eat um."

    —*Joshua Slocum (in Samoa),* Sailing Alone
      Around the World

DAN

DAY 317. The last day.

0500. I can feel Montauk, and I don't know if that's because I trust my navigation or if it's a feeling I have by itself. I *know* it's just over the curve of the earth.

Not wanting to round the point with a foul tide, I drift and sleep for a few hours. Then I put on too much sail and start beating toward home. The rail is constantly awash, but I don't care. *Sparrow* is crashing through waves, splashing sheets of spray twenty feet in all directions. I feel like a fluorescent light bulb trying to light. I want to just ease the sheet a bit and turn back to sea while there is still time, as at Fernando; but I'm out of chutney. Got to restock, at least.

Can I keep this dream going forever and never again face the consequences of human interaction? Where do I fit in and what do I do now? Am I still in my dad's shadow or can I go forward with this lead? Do I have my own permission? When will I know?

0700. Montauk. I sail close into the shore and tack up toward the point. The water is a frothy blue-green. It is different from any other water I've seen this past year.

1200. I pull out the radio and hear the voices of friends telling me to hurry up. There are seventy-five people waiting, and CBS can't wait past five o'clock. I cringe, then ease the sheet a wee bit, slowing down and sending CBS on their way.

As usual it's choppy—all of the ocean trying to squeeze into Long Island Sound by way of this point. I pick out familiar landmarks—the nuclear power plant, Race Rock, New London Ledge, New London Light. They all come out of the blur as they stood against the backdrop of my imagination for so long.

Two motorboats covered with cameras churgle out and find me. I am circled and clicked at—talk about self-conscious! I haven't dealt with more than three people at a time for ten months, and suddenly through their lenses I am presenting myself to millions! It's quite clear that tonight everyone on earth will stop what they're doing and watch me on television.

I sail past my home, which stands on four iron legs over the familiar piece of rock, Hobb's Island. The water is deep up to the front porch and I am tempted to jump off. The monkey looks at it sideways.

The motorboats with their camera crews are gone now (setting up their "arrival shots," I imagine). I see Burr's dock a mile north. It looks crowded.

Out of the familiar scenery roars Dad in our launch, *Rozinante*. It needs paint. He's all smiles. We give each other a silent look of love—we don't even wave.

Dad motors off to catch lines at the dock. It's very quiet. The wind's gentle and northeast, my favorite wind.

A half mile to go.

NOTES MADE in the bathtub, first week home:

Giving someone my autograph, I spelled my name wrong. Home is finding your old key chain and having no idea whose it is. I forget what the keys do. I'll have to start over!

One year. I don't judge it by one more income tax return, or another twelve months of screaming TV commercials. I see it as more than six hundred sun sights and the Earth's gone around again. I wasn't here to watch changes take place at home, and sailing is such another world that the past year seems like a movie that just let out. I've been gorging myself on everything craved—women, driving too fast, loud music, bread, baths, and clean clothes. I'm surprised to again find that happiness doesn't come from how much I can consume. It was easy to think so all year—that all that stuff would make a difference. I forgot it's why I left.

My checkbook is . . . well, it just is. I can't remember how to use it. My ears buzz from loud Rolling Stones music, and last weekend I dented the front of my car by driving too far into some backwoods of Maine.

My desire to do more and go farther hasn't changed one bit. And I know it never will. I won't stuff desires, or whims, or fantasies away with reasons to justify why I shouldn't pursue them. Sometimes I feel like Tiger on his morning spaz run.

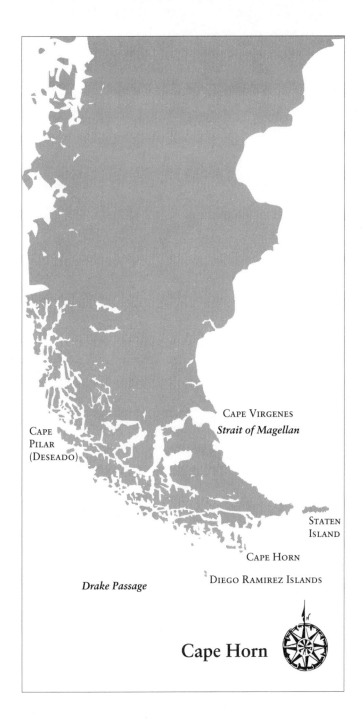

CAPE VIRGENES

Strait of Magellan

CAPE
PILAR
(DESEADO)

STATEN
ISLAND

CAPE HORN

DIEGO RAMIREZ ISLANDS

Drake Passage

Cape Horn

AFTER

DAVID

It is two and a half years since Dan came upriver to Burr's Yacht Haven, where reporters and about fifty of his friends were waiting, and where his carpentry students held up a sheet lettered WELCOME DAN. Now we're driving to Burr's in his tiny, rattling Jeep; he traded in a good car for the kind of spine-bruiser we rented on Easter Island. When he turns on the ignition, a concerto by Handel blares out. He's had it tuned to the classical music station. He snaps it off. "Damn kids break in and change the channel. Oh, by the way, Dad, I came across my old 'essential' list, and there was a leather punch on it. We never got one. I can't believe we made it around!"

"Dan, I've got bad news too. Our *Aku Aku* caught a leak from my office ceiling. It's pulp. Twice around The Horn and now this." I'd phoned Ty when I arrived home, and spoken to his wife. I'd asked, as delicately as I could, if he'd made it around. He had. "Where is he now?" I asked. "I don't really care," was the answer.

We've met to tow *Sparrow* down the Thames River after

repairs to a small nick in her keel. She moors in a cove next to our island home. It's quite rocky, and often there's time for only one grab at the mooring, which Dan missed after an afternoon sail. We do things like that from time to time; I had been current-swept under an unopened bridge not long before. We confess our mishaps to each other, concerned not to become ashamed or secretive about errors. "You're good sailors," my brother said, "but you need a lot of room."

We stop at the shoreside clammery/hamburgery. I try not to stare at Dan.

"Dad, stop staring at me."

"Sorry."

"You know, if we're going to write a book about the voyage, we've got to be heroic."

"You're right. I just read about this guy who hints at it a lot. He had to climb his mast in a real crooked ocean to re-rig his halyard."

"Yeah, we shouldn't have rigged three spares up there."

"What about being spies?"

"I thought of that, but I'd have to kill you."

"Dan, what about when you had to swim back to the boat in Drake Passage. That was heroic."

"Not really, I just wanted to get back on board. Anyway, the water was freezing."

"Vito Dumas broke his nose when he was off The Horn and went around all bloody."

"We shouldn't have made such good hand grips."

"Wouldn't have helped, he was sitting down. What about when we had to blow up the rubber dinghy by mouth?"

"Dad, we want to look like heroes, not idiots."

"What about when I fled from that raging bull on Santa Cruz?"

"That was a cow and she was walking the other way."

"I read all that Proust—*Remembrance of Things Past.*"

"Not macho, but you're getting warmer."

"What about our Thanksgiving meal, when we'd forgotten the cranberry sauce and I concocted it and it was good?"

"That's it! That was truly heroic, Dad."

"Thanks, Dan. But you were pretty great too."

Later, at Burr's, the river is quiet under a watermelon moon. I cast off *Sparrow*, Dan is alongside in *Rozinante* and takes the tow line. We start clowning, as usual.

"C'mon, Dad, *follow* me!"

"Hell, Dan, bring that thing in line ahead!" I pull the tiller handle out of the rudder post, walk forward and offer it to him.

Twilight thoughts, back in the tiny cockpit. This stretch of river recalls the segment of tape recorded for us by a friend from the eleven o'clock news, after Dan sailed the final mile of the voyage. *Sparrow* is beautiful, and there is a moment in the shot when Dan goes forward to set his bow line. She's so tiny when a human form takes the five or six steps of her length! The tape shows the champagne poured on his head, his clear face and direct and modest answers about courage and achievement. I recall how, in the few remaining minutes of useful afternoon light, one reporter and her cameraman came over to me.

She held out the microphone. "Do you think there are any other fathers as proud as you?"

My head goes down thoughtfully (confusedly) and then back up, down and up, and a fuzzy, "Well, no ma'am, I guess not." Leonora said later, "David, why didn't you just say, 'I hope so'?" Because—because I was thinking (a mistake during most interviews) of the men and women sent to war and families torn apart, the battlefields Dan and I have never been on, my friends just slightly older who were conscripted and died. I didn't say to the reporter, "Holy shit, lady, we were on a *yacht*. It was our *choice!*"

A racing-car driver, Sterling Moss, after a year in which

a dozen of his friends died, said that there is no such thing as courage, there is only compulsion or necessity. Leave it there. I've always believed he was right, and we had a hell of a ride.

Dan made it home in time for the wedding. He was the best man but looked, bluntly speaking, not his best in a suit and tie. He stood next to Julia and Jack, and Jack's two sisters, on the five-foot-square platform with its arched canopy that he and I had built the night before. A moment or two into the ceremony, tears started to stream down the tanned cheeks of my tough captain, and they weren't wiped away.

Dan's voyage gave him the resolve to be what his uneven academic skills had discouraged. He's back in school for an advanced degree in environmental studies. Each January 8 since our voyage, we've been together, and our ceremony, to mark the night we sailed from the Pacific back into the Atlantic, has been to stand dressed under a cold shower and toast again with a finger of Kahlua, "To the people who died here."

The voyage was more than I thought it could be. And, as always, the sea does not return what you ask for. You set out on her for adventure, but the strongest memory she grants you is the beauty of her moods. The Horn? All that I dreamed of was there, but my lifetime fantasy and its enactment have been moved aside by joy and pride at my son's achievement, bringing us around with such perfected skill and intuition, and his forty-two days alone.

Now Julia and Jack have given us a grandchild and nephew, and now I have the lengthened sense of being, as if life were one of those deep fissures in rock or an ice field that, with a child, you straddle and then, with a grandchild, you pull the other leg across and are safe on the far side.

A college roommate now known as Adam Smith wrote a handsome article about us for *Esquire*. In it, Smith asks,

"Why?" My answer is, "I've loved sailing so much I thought I owed something back to the ocean."

"David . . . said that sentence to me several times," Smith writes, "but I didn't get it. When I decided to write this piece, I asked him about it again, but he still couldn't explain it to me. Maybe some other sailor can."

But Smith says something that is equally hard for *me* to understand: how difficult it would be to spend so much time in such close proximity to one's father or son.

"I love you," I say aloud, and to my surprise there is an answer to my reverie. Dan turns in *Rozinante* and calls out over the sound of the outboard, "What'd you say, Dad?"

Did I yell? Did he see my lips move? "I love you," I shout, and without hesitation or awkwardness he calls back, "And I love you."

Now we're close to the mooring, and I think through the various ways we could pick its line out of the water. But I don't call to Dan; I know he'll do it well and that I'll instantly understand his scheme and do my part. And so it is. In silence the buoy is plucked up, the launch is out of the way and spun about, he hands me the line as *Sparrow* becomes still in the water. I secure her and we ride the few yards to the home we built.

Dan studies under the kerosene lamp; I check through a grant application. "Bet a million you can't read one page of this chemistry, Dad," he says. I try, and stumble over the fifth word. "Hah! That's only four million I owe you! And furthermore . . ."

"Oh, pipe down," I say. "I don't want to hear about that," and he resumes his study. I know he's right about the John Denver tape. I'm still too stubborn to give in. Let him read about it here.

We kiss and go to bed, but the oil light in his eight-foot-square loft is still warmly on above me when I fall asleep. We're up at six. "Coffee, Dan?" I'm at a stove that doesn't leap about.

"Yes, Dad, and I had a *great* dream!" He comes down the ladder and hands me a paper. He's written the dream for me. It is titled, "Dream on Island, Dad and Me," with the date.

It was perfect. The island was in Bahama-bright water. On the shore were white sand and relatives and friends, all happy.

Back from the beach was a forest of tall trees with a meadow. Farther back there were Vermont green hills—no houses—just hills. Beyond them a mountain range made from one upheaval, the striations of the sedimentary slabs uplifted and forming giant steps. On the top were snow and clouds and above the clouds the sky was blue like the water.

We went climbing on the biggest mountain. It was all sculptured gnarls like iron tree roots welded to slabs of stone and to strange furniture and chandeliers. All was one texture and one color, slate gray with white flakes.

We were equally young and strong, hauling each other up hand over hand. Sometimes there were no footholds at all, just our strong arms. On the top it was narrow, like the bronze *Alice in Wonderland* in Central Park.

At the very top was a chandelier fixture coming out of a ceiling from which the whole mountain grew, or hung, or they just met.

Now we were right at the top, hanging on and the plaster was pulling out. Dad wanted us to let go, to just fly off because it was a dream. I didn't want to in case it wasn't.

His hair was black, not white.

We held hands and floated off, laughing.

Well.

My own passage has taken place many times, when I am

wakeful at night, and I put my mind to a long swinging rhythm and imagine a moonbeam rolling through the room, a small oval of light shaped by one of the portholes we made. It curves and swings back. But the speaker is no longer my father.

Dad, I think I see The Horn.

It is my son.

APPENDIX

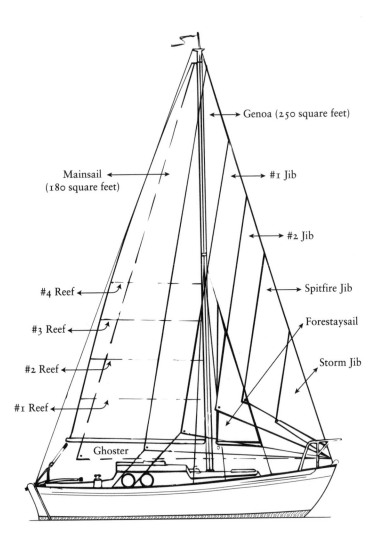

Genoa (250 square feet)

Mainsail
(180 square feet)

#1 Jib

#2 Jib

#4 Reef

Spitfire Jib

#3 Reef

Forestaysail

#2 Reef

Storm Jib

#1 Reef

Ghoster

Sample Log Entry,
approaching Cape Horn

The ship's log is, or should be, the ship's record and not our own journals. In it we enter matters relating to *Sparrow*'s business, and our errors, even embarrassing ones ("ran aground," etc.), must be recorded. But sometimes the ship should take note of major bathing activities, and so forth; and sometimes, well, there's a page to fill.

On the following two pages is the log for January 6, the twenty-second day out (upper left) on the passage from Easter Island to the Falklands. Sailors often do not put in their destination, which could be bad luck. At the end of the day we were 2,335 miles from Easter Island and only 253 from Cape Horn; our position at noon showed us deep in the Screaming Fifties.

To keep a little boat moving at her best, you tend to steer using the wind and seas to best advantage as they vary. That explains the different courses. The distances covered each hour are judgments by eye and are within a 5 percent error, as good as the mechanical odometer devices we could use.

The little triangles, like flags, indicate a sail change. The number 6 at the bottom of the left-hand page indicates that we made six changes that day, a relatively useless statistic. We also note our average speed, barometer readings (rising), and temperature.

On the right-hand page, note DDT (Dan, David, Tiger) as crew, and at the bottom we use the "Anchor Bearings" box to list our special tasks and repairs—Dan noted that he checked the foreguy and enlarged a safety harness. We did not note our water supply: we were abundantly stocked with fresh water, were sailing into a rainy area, and this was not one of our daily worries. I suppose it should have been —no portent of possible disaster should be overlooked.

DATE Sunday Jan 6 19.55   LOG OF YACHT

DAY 22   NOON 55°18's 73°51'N

| HOURS | COURSE by COMPASS | Error | Deviation | Distance by Log | Distance in Hours | WIND | | | TIDAL STREAM | | Barom'r | |
						Direction	Force	Leeway	Direction and Rate Knots	Allowance	Therm'r	
0 (Midnight)						▷	Jib.1	12.15				
1 (a.m.)	120 -¼			5		W	5-6	Brie-hi	moon	cleaR sky.		
2	120			5			OverCast, RAIN					
3	125			5								
4	110			5			DeRAIN but light					
5	115 #+5 118			6 22			LightRain				993	↑
6	100			5								
7	105			6		WSW	5-6				994	
8	110			6								
9	110' ↓			6 22		↓	↓					
10	120			6		↓	↓				995	
11	115			6	Dev Compass							
12 (Noon)	110			6	93	18°E. VAR (AVE 9.0R)					997	
13 (1 p.m.)	105			5							998	
14 (2 p.m.)	95			5								
15 (3 p.m.)	95			5							999	
16 (4 p.m.)	90			6		West - force 6-7						
17 (5 p.m.)	90			6		SW	5					
18 (6 p.m.)	100			6		WSW	6	1736 TurN JibToR #2◁	1002			
19 (7 p.m.)	100			5½			▷	1820 #2-Down				
20 (8 p.m.)	95			5½		WxS	5-6	▷ 1830 #2 reefort.				
21 (9 p.m.)	95			6						1004		
22 (10 p.m.)	100			6			▷2½ #2-Slab uP					
23 (11 p.m.)	100			6		▷ 2245 #2 Down ▷231 SAIL Flats.out						
(12 p.m.) 24 (Midnight)	100			5½		WxS	4-5					44°

Day's run 133 Nautical Miles (4-25½)   2335 42   3/6 1°c   Engine started
Time under way 24 h min   Engine stopped
Average speed 5.5 knots 8964   Engine running h min

FROM	....	H.W.	H.W.	H.W. ....
TO	....	L.W.	L.W.	L.W. ....
AT	....	H.W.	H.W.	H.W. ....
		L.W.	L.W.	L.W ....

TIDAL STREAMS at ....turn ....
at ....turn ....

DAILY REMARKS

CREW DOT

Finally a clear night (once-once) saw that to be west still duskish, moon coming up at low angle - 30° and due north by 0330 & it Full. Beautifull. Tug + 5/saft tender calls for long Time. Squalls later on & off and the brilliant discovery that I can stand on the Toilet and open the Fuevio hatch even in Rain (if from behind you stay dry) with the luxel phones on and make a pretty good ice berg, land, ship and while R.view. Letters & coffee. 0650 - Bright NW - overcast 10 mins later - in & out it goes. Moving easily & fast by 0700. Seas up from last night, but less confused, ship's motion easier. Brefast late, home & letters etc.

Barometer up & up. By noon we have cold & raw, mostly overcast, but enough sun for sights. Biscuits for lunch. Put position on 2 charts, frantic activity of sorts full of Triangles. Table slammings & dividers amidst Tiger Biscuits & lost pencils.

Fine afternoon: sail - Rorey. Finally (3 days) my long johns are dry enough to put away. Dri finally won big in our daily cri game. One albatries, 1 Petrel, (whaubirds). By 1700, 80% clear sky, fine weather, Bean & salmon supper. 1700, storm jib on, 1740 #2. Wind has veered to make reaching possible. By 1830, wind backed enough to blanket #2 - Brought it in & let out #2 reef of main. Seas big but easy 12-14' Sun down ± 2033. #2 Back up 2130, Fine moonrise, Jib slatting too much, down 2245. Moderating 2300, 2315 all main reefs out. 80% clear night - almost full moon. Cold - 44°, but dry air.

	FUEL — GALLONS/LITRES	FRESH WATER	ANCHOR BEARINGS
On Hand		3 with pieces	
Received		watch forecast	
Total		on large hand's	
Consumed			
Remaining			

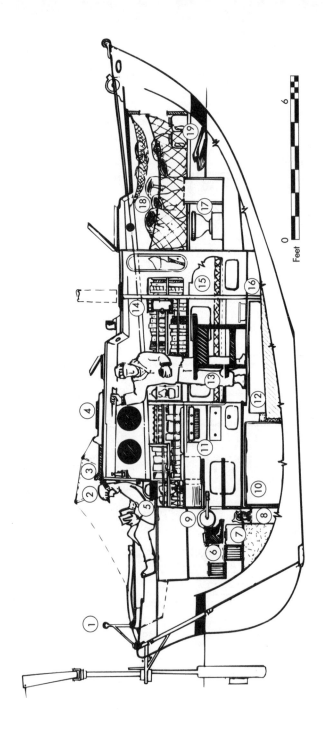

Feet

0

6

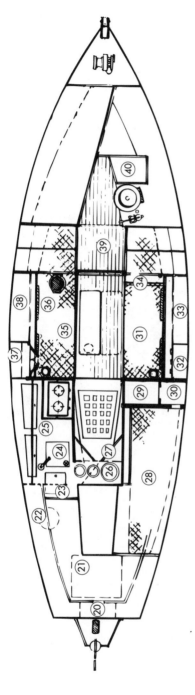

Interior of *Sparrow*

1. Main horse
2. Reading light
3. Spray dodger
4. Solar charging panels
5. Main compass
6. Storage batteries
7. Kerosene tank
8. Bilge
9. Bilge and sink pump
10. Main water tank
11. Stove

12. Second water tank
13. Below-deck compass
14. Cabin heater
15. Cave below vestibule cupboards, for feet when sleeping and bedding storage when awake
16. Anchor chain (at sea)
17. Head (toilet)
18. Larger sails, small hammocks for gear (port and starboard)
19. Anchors
20. Tiller locker

21. Lazarette hatch and lazarette
22. Emergency pump (under deck)
23. Icebox
24. Sink
25. Food lockers
26. Dish rack
27. Steps
28. Quarter berth
29. Foul-weather gear
30. Small-gear lockers
31. Starboard berth (Dan's), with food storage underneath

32. Radio
33. Navigation books, almanac
34. Bookshelf
35. Port berth (David's), with paint, fiberglass repair materials, and food underneath
36. Seat backs, which open for clothes storage (port and starboard)
37. Spices, galley items
38. Books
39. Vestibule
40. Vegetable bin

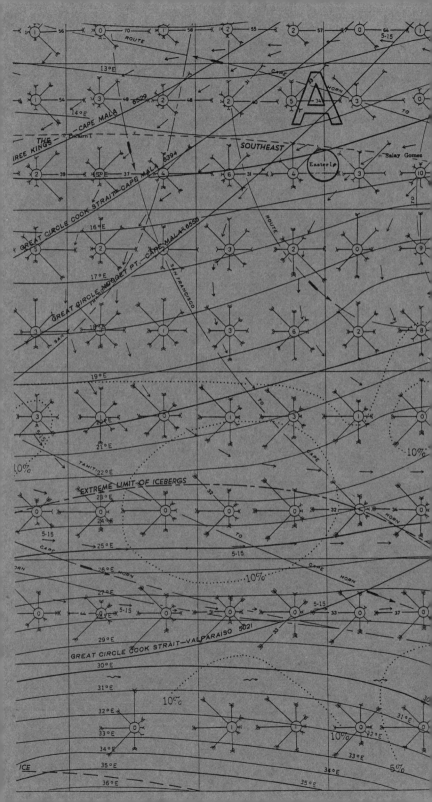